TEA

PARTY-

UNIVERSITY

A historic journey & vision to reform the broken California and U.S. public education system, from kindergarten to the historically corrupt CSU Stanislaus. Where the president, faculty and staff have obstructionist Tea Party affiliations!

A True Story by,

Roger "George" de Almeida

Rogerio "George" de Almeida

ISBN:1477493867
ISBN-13:978-1477493861

DEDICATION

This book is dedicated to Anita and John Kornfeld. To Anita my BFF and best selling novelist, and to John Kornfeld a great Artist, teacher and human being. I have the pleasure knowing and loving both of you dearly and forever

CONTENTS

This novel is about the public school education and the more illusive dream through the ladder of success. Some History of the civil rights movements all the way to the 99% movement is mentioned and focused on. Included are a few common sense ideas how to repair our broken educational system and democracy.

ACKNOWLEDGMENTS

Tolerance.org

Michelle Kwee

The state boy's rebellion

Red Cherry Day!

Almeida & Fred Boyce

Simon and Schuster

CBS NEWS

VIACOM

Anita and John Kornfeld

Those dirty bastards

Jim Crow laws

ALEC

Flying Tigers

Mr. Hee

Martin Luther King

Big Ed Shultz

Nixon

Kent state

UC Davis

Bush #41 & 43

Dick Chaney

President Kennedy

Governor jerry Brown

S.F. Portuguese Consulate

Senator Steinberg

Bonus army

Paul Ryan

Mad Max

Brad Pitt

CHAPTER ONE

"Elementary teaching & methods"

The original act and law of public education in the United States was started in Boston, "the Massachusetts Act of 1642." Started by the early settlers of this great country U.S.A... The law of 1642 was laid into law to contribute to the dream of social harmony via education of religion and literacy.

This was also the mandatory start of Harvard College "the true Tea Party University" in 1647. This law was implemented out of necessity, for if you can't understand or read, how else will the citizens be able to abide by the laws and rules of a growing society?

The growing parental negligence to educate there own children were a big problem then also. The same issues the teacher's use as an excuse for there failing poverty stricken parents and students to this day.

Also this was the same reason Thomas Jefferson proposed a bill for "common school movement in 1779." The reforms only took hold in the 1830'sThats fifty years of political red tape.

The key to the common school movement was to hire qualified teachers to educate the future citizens of our country and to help stamp out poverty. The story puts light that teachers blame the problems of today's student's drop out and failure rate are the parents fault!

The whole reason to star the public educational system was to educate the poverty stricken. Also the work load was horrendous and most parents did not have the time or means to educate their own children.

Anyone can learn! It is the methods in which the teacher uses. Also the demeanor and time spent demonstrating while teaching is essential and makes all the differences in the world.

It is hogwash and nothing more than an excuse to say it is the parent's fault the children are not learning.

My public education started at Seventh Street School in San Pedro, California in 1969 and is part of the Los Angeles unified school district. Neither of my parent's finished high school or spoke more than a few words in English back then.

They both managed to have great jobs and a great middle class life. More than half of my fellow classmates were also from many different ethnic groups and had similar childhoods as myself. I watched my father work his way up from Los Angeles public housing to the American dream he came here for, the work ladder to the middle class and the road out of poverty.

My father always worked very hard even many double shifts for years. He loved the respect he got for the great work he performed over the many years. He worked for all big corporations most are still very famous brands to this day.

My father Jose's first big step out of poverty was purchasing a10 unit apartment building in Long Beach, California. My father worked very hard to achieve his American dream as did I. He also worked hard for the financial stability of his large family.

I was born on December 3rd 1964 to Portuguese immigrant parents. My mother Lucia is from historically rich Lisbon. My father is from a small fishing village in Sisembra.

Portugal is one of the countries directly involved in discovering America and was the first makers of maps in the world. Portugal started out centuries ago as a Monarchy ruled government until the 20th century. Then the country was under strict dictatorship rule by Salazar until the civil revolution of April 25th 1974 when Portugal became a young Democracy.

Just like Tea Party member Senator Marco Rubio my parents are true exiles from their home country. Portugal was a dictatorship when my parents left for France. They migrated to France, then Canada and then to California to stay until 2003.They retired American citizens and moved back to the new young democratic Portugal.

I am the youngest of five children and my mother Lucia worked for TWA at Los Angeles international airport, in catering. My father Jose worked for a famous tuna brand cannery on Terminal Island in L.A. harbor.

My family took part in the economic building and the shaping of the true American democracy we all should love and promote more for this country. Portugal is just like a large percentage of small countries around the world that were, and are currently governed by real socialists, communists, dictatorships, monarchies and oligarchies and combinations thereof and some are disguised as a democracy.

True democracy itself is what the United States of America is really used to being associated with and stood for around the world. True civil democracy is considered to be the real true American dream. Protests in the sixty's and seventy's were a fight for more than civil inequality the fight was also for economic inequality.

Martin Luther king started the civil rights movement and I am sure he would have told you economic inequality itself was actually a big part of the movement then too. GOP Senator West is fabricating history as all Tea Party politicians seem to do in today's political theater.

This was one large bit of American history I was fortunate of witnessing first hand. Not only did I see them in person when I went somewhere with my parents, the protests were on TV almost daily back then.

The fight for true democracy with economic Equality is being protested yet again in our immediate history with the 99% movement. This is the real movement of "We the People."

The Tea Party movement was made up by the ALEC, The heritage foundation and other organizations using patriotic names to confuse us with there plan to end democracy altogether.

This Ideology is directly funded by the 1% to make us fall into their misguided Ideologies that are archaic and is trying to erase the true democracy in this great country of ours history.

I also believe my parents wanted to reach the one percent and aimed for that current dream. My parents with many years of working in the U.S. accomplished with speaking very little English.

They would simply bring one of us children along to read, translate and speak for them as many immigrants still do to this day. My parents also had us fill out checks to pay all the different family bills throughout the years.

My parents both worked hard and my fathers dream was to buy and give each of his kids a house to live out our years. My parents bought several properties in the early 1970's to further their American dream.

By 1976 my parents worked and achieved purchasing three beautiful houses in San Pedro and the apartment house in Long beach. A very good indication that anyone, even people who did not speak very much American English in this developing country; could work towards the American dream and all that it entails.

That also entails the strengthening of the work ladder that is currently at a real risk of ending as is our civil rights. The biggest and best part of this country's history is the building of true democracy itself.

The other big part of the building of this country was the huge immigration of manpower needed for such endeavors for the building of what we call the United States of America.

That huge migration is what helped propel and build this country to the superpower status it is today. It was the all the different hearts and minds of the immigrants who dreamed of that prized ticket to America that made it what it is today.

This infusion of manpower was a vital key to making America one of the world's destinations for dream realizations and the superpower it is today. The Vietnam War was also on every mind, people were still building fall out shelters out of nuclear war fears that did not go away totally from the cold War era.

President Kennedy was assassinated that sad day in June 1969. By November Nixon won the 1970 presidential election with a platform of "Law and Order". This also was part of the Democracy building and human rights strengthening in this anti war era.

Nixon and his "law and Order" presidential election platform of 1970 put our country in a "Chemical War" that no one knew about in Cambodia until 14 months later.

The students from Kent State University protested the War; tricky Dick had the National Guardsman open fire on the protesters, as in the recent Oakland, California 99% protesters.

Nixon said he deplored the guardsman actions but also said "when dissent turns to violence it invites tragedy." Well Nixon should have listened to the protesters instead of throwing tear gas canisters that inspired rock throwing retaliations.

Deception to start War was used in recent history again by the other tricky Dick; Chaney and Bush's Iraq War Watergate to make themselves and their cronies much, much richer with taxpayer's money "the middle classes money".

Norquest worked for Nixon and learned all of his antics and governing tactics then. How could one person's contract of ideology cripple a country?

I am proud to be a part of the experiences that added too our country's true democracy. Watching history unfold made me open my eyes to other ways of critical thinking throughout my educational life. You simply have to imagine yourself being that object or person or whatever it may be.

For example slavery; the reason it was abolished is that some people in this democracy felt that the slaves were equal people too. Black, White or Yellow it doesn't really mater because we are just as human and we bleed the same as the next person. I also learned that I was a "neoconservative back then" along the way of learning our political system and human rights history in this period of my childhood.

I witnessed democracy at its rawest form as did Dylan Ratigan with the first Wall Street 99% protesters in a New York City park a few months ago. I feel the Occupy movement is for more than just civil rights and economic equality. It is history in the making of democracy strengthening that is better for our growing country.

I want to emphasize "growing country". Clearly I am remembering that the schools back then were full of the same challenges and more difficult ones as they are facing today. Some good and bad things came out of the newly mandatory integrations of the time.

We as students for the most part were eager to end the segregation of the United States public education system and really start learning the standard public school curriculum of the time.

All these constant big changes in the building of democracy made us a much stronger nation. What needs to be done today, besides a huge system wide overhaul of United States banking and election processes?= Adapting new laws that help implementations of a better society is a big part of building our true democracy and we need this desperately.

I haven't seen protests for civil fairness and jobs as large as the Wall Street 99% protesters since my childhood. Throughout time democracy, as it is today is being tested again. The Tea party movement seems not to take science and our growing population and they need to govern for such changes in mind but we know they can but the greed for money no mater who suffers.

We need to stay as a true government of democracy and think and plan ahead for the needs of citizens as our population grows this is what a real democratic government itself should entail.

This feat is apparently, still a work in progress I truly hope. Although true democracy takes looking ahead and governing that way must be done also. We started seeing in the 1960's; what was happing in the reconstruction years and the new "Jim Crow laws."

This is the same as the Radical Republicans "the modern day Tea Partiers." They are starting the same ideological War today but now instead of blacks only; it is now for all the poor citizens no mater who or what color you happen to be!

This rehashed GOP ideology; all being done for pure greed to enrich themselves and their Wall Street cronies in this man made gilded age to the infamous 1%. This greed has also entered in the Democratic Party due to the election auction and needs to be rectified fast, for the good of the United States of America and the freedom we should still stand for.

It was a newly felt feeling growing up on the new highways built for new jobs and our growing countries infrastructures sake. It worked then and as all the things we learned from history it will work again. I remember going for a drive down Pacific Coast Highway in my dad's cool 289 ford galaxy wood paneled wagon looking at all the new billboard advertising along the way.

And wow did it ever create a significant amount of new businesses along the newly built highways. Back then there were the big nice new highways being constructed everywhere in Los Angeles and throughout the America I love?

This same dilemma is what the GOP and some other political parties of today think we could not afford to do today. "I say we cannot afford not to invest in our future!" China is and more than half of Chinas population can't even monetarily afford to use it themselves yet! "Due to the very large slave population needed for their cheap labor market they created & cultivated"

Although the *Jacksonians; the Tea Party of NO to the railroad expansion of the 1800's.* That great vision of our fore fathers George Washington, Lincoln also governed for the future United States.

This is the true American way and what the fore fathers did see for this awesome county we call the United States of America. They defiantly had the future in mind as they were drafting our Country's doctrine the United States Constitution over two hundred thirty five years ago. The Tea Party of today just doesn't seem to understand or just don't care to understand our countries true history.

It seems the Tea Party felt it was necessary to using the bully type confrontations of my public school days and use them in our politics of today. This type of governing is now on the news and going on in our congress daily. It was out of control back then and seemed to have fixed it for a couple decades but here we are again.

Like that old cliché says "history has a way of repeating itself" and not only for this era. This 1960's early 1970's era stepped up the strengthening of our countries democracy and GDP and was detrimental to the contentment of our civil society.

This investment in our infrastructures made our country and its citizens wealthier at a more even American Dream playing field then today. This reason is why the touchy civil rights subjects are becoming such a big controversy again today.

All our American lives were all changing for common good and fair civil rights goals it felt great even at my age back then. The protests made the politicians put these problems to debate and then to the congress. They debated the new problems for a bipartisan outcome that helped "We the People"; that is just a part of what democracy itself is in this country.

The protests themselves made this country the democracy powerhouse it is today. A forced early education on discrimination and different forms of preferential treatment by the politicians and teachers back then was a factor in the drop out statistics then, as it is today for the most part.

The educational road ahead was just getting more difficult for some raciest teachers, administrations and students. There was obvious special treatment for most kids. That mostly came out of the PTA "parent teacher association".

It was normal then and was an early form of profiling and the sizing up of a particular student parents. It was also used widely by the teachers that result in unfair grading policies and discrimination for the other students. These discriminations are apparently still going on today and also have to change.

Teachers that take the time necessary to give that extra caring practices individually is also used for the kids whose parents had the means and time to meet with the teachers were treated very different from the other student's parents who did not have the time or means to be there for whatever their reasoning.

The preferential grading also statistically favors the females especially by the female teachers. For years teachers have been issuing good grades and bad grades without someone overlooking this practice! Also teachers doing the due diligences of what the child actually know not a multi choice test but a short written answer test before, during and after the instructional year.

Then instead of giving those failing grades to the slower learning students or a passing grade just because of age. Special classes that make sure they are actually learning should be able to take these kids and create a new pace of learning for those kids in the same school.

Instituting new teaching practices should be part of the new reform of school curriculums today. Like the no child left behind that President Bush started years back is a complete failure.

It was due to the bad implementation of the flawed idea. This especially occurred to the low income areas portion of the school districts. This is what started the teacher to pad grades. And in some well known cases the teachers padded test results for the sake of the schools budget they work for. Or was it the continued GOP Tea Party ploy to end education for the lower class citizen?

Just as schools today our public schools were full of reasons to love and hate going to school. The politics of the individual school districts policies is and was half the battle for a balanced educational experience.

Also we must put an end to the different kind's discrimination just because of the child's skin differences. It even happened to me again recently in Gov. Brown's office by the sheriff out side who let me in. He then came back to the waiting area to interrogate me!

These same budget buster practices need to be dropped from teaching practices altogether. This alone would show results for a great well rounded less expensive education.

One of the great reasons to go to school was the enjoyment to learn new and different things no matter what the subject. This learning style is called Interpersonal- talking and working together.

Another learning style there is called Intrapersonal- thinking and doing alone during a quite time. Then the Visual approach to teaching-illustrations like graphs, drawings, flowcharts both looking in the book and the actual making of flowcharts.

Also we can use the Analytical learner's method-How does that work? For learners who need to have the details before the big picture by working on one section of the book at a time until it makes sense.

Also a global learner's method-"why does that work?" Yet another learning method is the Kinesthetic-movement and doing-"study by using objects and motions".

Next one is the auditory method -"listening to tapes and or plays music while studying or taking notes on a tape recorder."

Not to forget the normal Verbal method-"talking method learning while being explained or described something."

All subjects instructed in a fun and critical thinking oriented ways in a K thru 6th grade public school situation is optimal. This would allow for a lifetime of great learning techniques for all classes of students. These learning enhancement tools allows for a healthier growing mind also.

The instituting of new teaching methods introduces the students to critical thinking concepts at an early age. This is critical for the future K-6 students and for the path of success for using this better method of teaching in the early years of life.

This new multi interaction and educational type of stimulation would enrich every single student that walked in the class door no mater what social class the student was born too.

This style of teaching will also help the different public and private educational institutions keep there costs down for a great education. It will defiantly create a more gratifying learning experience for both the teacher and student. This can be done by implementing all teaching methods in a day of instruction everyday. Weather it was making the subject exciting or giving the subject a real life comparison that would spark in our minds.

All that inciting fun instruction processes in the same period and on whatever the subject being taught. This new method I modeled from many individual methods is essential to a great day of learning.

Teachers that have a knack for making the individual student interested and the class as a whole all in the same period is a great teacher. Teachers should be allowed to take all the different learning styles we now know and implement them. This would overhaul the current public one size fits all "teach for test" education system that is clearly not working.

This investment of critical thinking techniques intergraded with other traditional methods of teaching should be in our new curriculums now. In return we will keep the dropout rate much lower and GPA grade point rates up. This new method also makes keeping students interested in learning and certainly will have a positive impact on all students.

Everyone should have great memories of all teachers they had and remember all their names, not just one or two. The teachers that did not make learning easier and perhaps fun for yourself are the teacher's names that are not in your current memories of your educational lives history right?

Now you possibly can see how it would increase the educational value of each day of the student and the teacher in the very important educational journey we call school.

This upgraded teaching method at the developing stages of students would also solve some of the other problems that arise in an educational system. This should be the future of American public schools and private.

The Professors in Colleges and Universities seem to think a lot of students who are remedial throughout the K thru 12th grades fall through the cracks or has no higher educational dreams.

"I challenge that blame it on the cracks garbage." I believe through my early school experiences that some students do fall off the public school teaching train tracks.

But that whole premise is only true if the teachers don't have the teaching tools needed for a great leaning atmosphere needed to learn effectively. For that reason the analogy of train tracks is defective as the teachers that believe it is a normal outcome for some students.

CHAPTER TWO

"Developing minds and values"

The human brain grows and develops faster in the K-6 critical learning years and is only derailed by using the current "teaching the test" instruction. These new federal guidelines produced by the Bush administrations "leave no child behind" law.

This law seems to be having a total opposite outcome for the young students. This is partially due to the pressure added to teachers for federal money for the school and or district they work for.

The current broken educational system needs to be overhauled with solutions and the same needs to done to our current broken government. "We the people" have and know what's truly good for a healthy and fair social democracy in this country, especially now.

The beginning years in any life is the critical learning period that is very important to a well developing and functioning brain. This critical time is also the perfect time to engage in critical thinking techniques we can teach.

The new things learned and the eye opening type of learning experiences will certainly last a lifetime. The other great school experiences I remember are the things the students learn from other classmates, like on "show and tell days" for example.

I remember the other kids and I would come to class on those days with something from home. Then we would have to go up to the front and face the whole class and tell our story about whatever we brought.

This one traditional teaching technique is a keeper and works. It teaches many students different lessons other than the regular subjects thought in the classroom.

The food pyramid nutritional program was very good and needed program. It was also started in the early 1970's it worked but was flawed. The only problem the program had is it was taken out of the yearly curriculum to soon.

It should be continued and introduced in all 6th-12th grades, because a good traditional start to well balance nutritional education that would have lasted a lifetime. This in itself would have had a much greater impact on the growing obesity rate of the recent decades we have had without it.

There is a whole curriculum in the university system to teach proper nutritional habits why not keep it part of our curriculums for K-12th grade. Both the nutritional program curriculum implemented in the early 1970's along with the presidential physical education program is winners. Both of the programs of that era should be continued and expanded beyond the third grade.

The problem with our public school education curriculum is that the great learning methods and ideas, are not being implemented in our current curriculums in a common sense way.

The early days of my public education were also the height of the corporal punishment movement in the public school system. Teachers felt it was there right to swat or hit a student as they saw fit, supposedly "for class control."

This was another way the power as a teacher strengthened and was wrong and miss used in many overreaching ways.

There was such a public outcry and lawsuits that put an end to this self ruled and often abused law for the teachers. I personally had seen things I still remember vividly.

There is one event in particular that came back to haunt me recently because my current CSU nightmare situation. This CSU situation made me want to expose all the U.S. educational issues I know "first hand" to the world.

I had a classmate, a guy named John. All our fellow classmates called him "snots". A good part of the kids back then as nowadays were bullies or sided with one. The problem was much worse then that I believe it is now and the problem is really bad now.

John had allergy and mucous problems and came to school with the same dirty clothing for days. John was not from an immigrant family as I. John spoke American English very well and was his only language.

I became his friend not because others were afraid too, but for I knew John to be a great normal kid. I believe he was a foster child and seemed to be poor. Looking back, he was powerless and was just too young too do anything about the abuse and discrimination he received at Seventh Street School by this unforgettable teacher!

One day John was particularly dirty and had some dried mucous on his face "more than usual." The teacher grabbed his hand and pulled his whole body out of his one piece desk. I was horrified as she grabbed that ugly paddle and slapped his butt hard as she could. "I can't believe that was allowed by law those days".

She was doing this simultaneously while dragging him to the far corner of the classroom. I will never forget the horror! And it took place in elementary school. After that huge scene she created she yelled to him to "stay there until he stopped crying".

John at that point had a large amount of tears and snot coming out of his eyes and nose. This supposedly was her problem with him in the first place? Her picking on him always left him even much dirtier the rest of his day; not to mention his recollections of the temple squeezer. Most of the other kids were laughing and some were as scared as I was.

I can still hear her yelling at him and spanking him with that whole ridden wooden paddle, as John was being dragged to the corner of the classroom. I recall that the whole class was all afraid of her in one way or another. Especially that paddle; the temple squeezer loved to use almost daily. The paddle hung on a nail next to the left entrance of the classroom.

One day miss Bean my forth grade teacher came in from her class next door and asked the temple squeezer "what was all that fuss was about?" and that temple squeezer lied and said John had fallen down. I will never forget that sad day and what the teacher got away with! John and my innocence and the others were lost that day.

This particular paddle looked homemade. It was a wooden paddle and was about 30 inches long and about 5 inches wide and at least an inch thick. Black tape was rolled thickly around the raw cut handle. This paddle was riddled with drilled out holes. I will never forget that paddle as long as I live, and I never saw one like that since.

That teacher would squeeze the student's temples too. I can't seem to remember her by her real name; she was so mean I just called her the temple squeezer. When I get a headache I still usually think of that morally challenged teacher the temple squeezer "because she did it to me too" I now think of Professor Shou Wang and the corrupt CSU Stanislaus in the very same way.

The recollections that I am writing are about some real life experiences of my educational life. Starting from my very 1st grade class. My public education also came with another real life education on different forms of racism and discrimination.

The continued use of preferential treatments that some teachers use as teaching methods often to this day are wrongly used. "Some without knowing there was doing it visibly." Teaching is a supposed noble profession but it is infected by child abusers even today as in the Penn state ordeal "Another corrupt school." Some of those school days are really sad but eye opening never the less.

I also remember some other scary days the temple squeezer was teaching. The class assignment was to make a turquoise necklace out of clay chunks and turquoise and black paint. John had to sneeze and he had a long strand of mucus hanging out of each of both his nostrils.

Instead of the temple squeezer handing him a tissue paper, witch she did after yanking him and swatting him with that big ugly paddle again. One day the temple squeezer did it again and this time I could not just sit there and watch her cruelty and moral less abuse on John.

I honestly know that he really never said or did; nor I did anything to receive such abuse. "I sat next to him" Nothing that he did warranted the treatment or violence used on him by the teacher.

"Showing up to school grungy" I still believe the temple squeezer just did not like him period. Or did his appearance of being dirty really make her paddle him constantly?

I also assure you he was afraid of her, I recall he would start crying before she even got close to him. "That would make her even more upset at John." I can still see her big black bulging eyes. Her nose also flared out like a "wild boar."

I spent years trying to figure a good reason for her evilness growing up. As I am writing these recollections, my eyes are welling up and I still come up empty for excuses for her. I can only recall seeing her as the moral less inhumane temple squeezer and not as a teacher.

Also I vividly recall getting in the way of that paddle and John one rainy afternoon. My eyes are tearing up not just because I am reliving that moment, but I also recall getting struck by that whole ridden paddle that really hurt.

After that day I got in the way of the temple squeezer and John. Her paddle time treatment was altered from then on "I was being abused as was john." To this day I wonder what ever happened to John.

I also wonder about the other children that teacher abused over the years? Did she hurt one to many students and finally got reprimanded or fired before, the end of the unfairly used corporal punishment laws of that era?

As the youngest out of five children and was used to standing up for myself at a very early age. Well for me getting intimidated by the normal psychological garbage that bullies and older siblings try to get away with. Well those behaviors just get me upset to this day.

I feel privileged to grow up in Los Angels, California and called it home for many years. History was unfolding in school and on television every day from civil rights to the first space launching in the Mohave Desert.

I watched sadly as many did, President Kennedy getting assassinated and the Vietnam War protests. Growing up in Los Angeles in this era, as it turned out was a great history lesson in itself.

I was a good kid generally, a well loved normal kid that lived for adventures at a young age and still do. I loved going fishing with my friends at ports o call village. Riding bikes all over San Pedro and watching T.V. shows and movies being filmed off Gaffey Street in San Pedro, like the Mod Squad, Adam Twelve and others.

I also loved to watch Superman, Spiderman, Felix the Cat and other comic reels before cable T.V. was invented. Also the choices of toys were not what they are today so the toy industry was just beginning to be a booming new industry.

The same with learning devices and toys that are available to parents and teachers these days that were not readably available back then. For the most part kids from the 1960's era loved to play more outdoors and were statistically more active then the kids of today.

It was the new jobs created by companies and innovations that came with the masses of citizens working in the "infrastructure" producing government. These protocols are all being implemented by our then government. This was all created for a common future, and the building of millions of jobs.

This government regulated processes also allowing for a decent wage that gave new buying power to ordinarily poor citizens created new wealth and bigger industries. Much needed new changes to our laws to allow the necessary investment for the current growing population.

It was a huge commitment to true democracy then. It is currently desperately needed again now for the rebuilding and strengthening of our own American government.

Without a truly democratically run government that really cares for this nation's ordinary citizen and its changing laws and regulations, we would not be the superpower that we are today.

It feels and looks like the American dream was more in reach back then that it is currently. This is just one bit of our country's history the Tea Party just doesn't seem to grasp. Besides that part of our U.S. history it seems to rewrite others as it seems fit. This too seems to be the new GOP Tea Party's obvious governing method or lack thereof.

My family along with many other newly immigrated families or people that came to this great country came for a better life, and focused on the American dreams of there own. My parents had worked very hard for years to achieve the now more illusive ladder of American success.

For my dad's pursuit he purchased three rental homes in San Pedro and one apartment building in Long Beach, California. This made us and everybody considered out large family to be middle class.

Rogerio "George" de Almeida

CHAPTER THREE

"LIVING THRU HISTORY"

Most of the student population in K-6th grade in my school English was a second language. In California, Arizona, New Mexico and Texas this is still a major social and education concern that continues today. This country was built on immigration and so the student populations grew rapidly also.

This was noticeable at all K- 12 schools and colleges I attended in the U.S. including CSU Stanislaus in Turlock Calif. For once again in years, people had extra money to spend and it felt good to be in America. Anyone working could finally afford luxuries that only the rich could afford in the past.

Things like transportation and traveling, farming for the masses and creating more exports. It was the expansion of Infrastructures such as new highways built and industry to accommodate Jobs for the increase in our growing countries population.

The building of factories that filled the stores with items we were proud to spend a little more on for that "Made in America" stamp. President Bush Jr. and his deregulation tactics and that old GOP trickle down garbage. They used fear and continue to do so for political restructuring that will end our democracy itself.

It will end what we as a nation has been struggling for since we started this country 236 years ago in 1776 "equality for all". The newly created GOP deregulations and what the Wall Street barons lobbied for resulted in fifty Thousand yes more than 50.000 MADE IN USA factories closed in this country in the eight years the GOP ideologies snuck by us in the name of security!

That when the "private parts" Dick, Bush, and Colon was in office. The Bay Bridge in San Francisco currently being built got the sell out the made in China stamp!
It really it came to this? OMG!

We have our own steel factories don't we? When did our own country's infrastructure have to with international trade? Or maybe it was a perk for an extra large loan we needed to finance that needless Iraq war incentive?

Now the GOP Tea Party wants and changed more laws that deregulates more of what "we the people" want for our country and our government. The system worked as did glass steagle did for over seventy years. This problem is going on for over two decades now and currently one of the biggest problems America and the free world democracy is facing again.

The Tea Party seems to believe our country is having this problem again because of what President Obamas has done in the last three years. The American government proved that when our country is governed for the masses it can propel the U.S. and the economy for the greater good as I explained earlier they did in the past.

This past thought full governmental actions not only raised the GDP, that methodical government action is what got us out of the big depression. This was done by a huge bipartisan multi trillion dollar investment in today's dollars. We need a huge expanding of our country's deteriorated and outdated infrastructure again now.

We are facing that situation again today for the most part. It was an infrastructure building campaign being implemented by our Government and then GOP President Eisenhower # 34.

Now President Eisenhower was a true republican. He was one of the modern era democracies visionary. He wanted and ended the stalemate Korean War. He also stopped corruption. He and his administration governed for the well being of our country. Also, as I saw it he governed for population increases and the capitalism growing government implementations at its best.

The only thing he did was that he liked Nixon and kept him on the ticket because of his views towards communism. So he looked the other way on his other dishonest political goals. This is before the tea party got a strangle hold on the GOP and why I was a neo conservative growing up in the 1970's.

That and other great ideas were invented and started for the Well-being of our countries growing population and the future democracy building and capitalism efforts of our former government. Something we must do now yet again to keep our superpower in tact. I believe in the threat from being overtaken by China if we don't do something proactive about it now.

The use of drones we invented and they replicate as all our other United States intellectual knowledge. For instance the Automobile, T.V., radio, solar, aircraft and now aircraft carriers and on and on and this is just China!

"We the people" need to voice our opinions and concerns in this big conundrum we put ourselves in. This problem we dug into is the direct result with big money in politics and the pandering and jerry rigging that happens on both sides of the isle and the big money corrupted administrations. We can start overcoming the inevitable now. This could be done by implementing what I call "save the free world" campaign.

I have been a die hard republican most of my life "and still love a few" but that has all recently changed as did the GOP. The Tea Party Bullies brinkmanship and current congress "just vote no" establishment. I vividly remember Regan and Nixon running for president. They both are from Los Angeles area. Mr. Norquest has too much power for an unpatriotic idiot who hides behind our great flag as many do these days.

I also remembered the day Kennedy and Martin Luther King were assassinated. I grew up watching the Vietnam War and U.S. in the space war the only War that was really worth bleeding for and winning along with the fight for equal rights for all citizens of our democracy.

The assassinations of the historical figures were nothing more then GOP fanatics wanting what the Tea Party has been getting away with recently. "The example" of a the recent political shooting of the congress woman Gifford's in Arizona that was incited by Sarah Palins caught in crosshairs hate campaign rederick.

The underlying and the huge problem we need to face and find a solution is the "keep the money out" campaign by Dillon Ratigan. The 99% Occupy movement also has been pinpointing all our problems lately. It found out it is that Wall Street IPO, junk sales and derivatives and worthless derivatives and fraudulent mortgage markets.

The current laws allows the Banks and the stock market barons and their cronies regulate themselves. "We the people" are all seeing what this corruption in our own government is doing to this country. The current career politicians are money blind and we continue to back the scams that got us to the brink of depression again.

The banks are self regulating and spreading the wealth clearly unfairly and true Americans with good morals can't stand it any longer. The lobbyists and big corrupt self regulating laws that the big banks and corporations pay for in an action type bidding situation even worse.

"Begging For more money to institute a new law of there choice" quid pro; but totally legal "just for them." They are and have been buying there own rules and the deregulations of laws. The Tea Party and it sneaky legislations canceled out a major banking law that worked since 1933 it was called Glass steagle.

This 1933 law got us out of the deep depression. The dismantling of this regulation is what started the world's current unreliable tensions to the world economic future. This is only one law that A.L.E.C. and Mr. McCarthy the deli owner, one more corrupting thing the Tea Party GOP got away with doing to the world besides a needless war that killed and maimed many people.

Including personal thoughts from some of our own young U.S. solders. The new GOP Government is to dismantle the free world as we know it for the ideology that was tried many for many years. It did not work then and it will never work!

Over recent years as the laws that was created to dismantle and shift the fifty thousand plus factories that left this country since 2001. We as a nation must continue hammering this into our new politics. We must reinstate ALL of the deregulations in the past twelve years!

The GOP Tea Parties 2006 congressional deregulation of government laws and giveaway to the rich tax incentives and loopholes that were bought too and caused millions of lost jobs. These tax incentives were created by the Wall Street Barons and lobbyists to give the companies they represent a bigger part of the monopoly of selling off paper junk. The GOP congress also created this huge man made problems we are facing in our government today.

The cause of millions of job losses of the last ten years, is because of what the GOP ideology and deregulating of the laws that use to work. You can ague that Even if they did not work to great it was much better than now that further deregulation happened.

The studies show the GOP is constantly trying to make the government smaller. The evidence shows at the same time they ran this country for years our government more than doubled! What rank hypocrisy!

Now they are doing the same with the United States Post office for example. In 2006 during the GOP lame duck session, they passed a law that the U.S. post office must fund the pensions of there workers many years in advance.

Now what company on this planet is required to do that? ONLY The U.S. Post office our congress saw to that law passing. The truth is; It is actually solvent the same as social security just not to the GOP Tea Party.

The Jim Crow laws reversal and other undemocratic and corrupt type of laws instituted for the oppression of "We the People" of the United States of America.

I personally want to know why the government is trying to make this country a third world type of country. I believe it is the privatization of the prisons that are primarily owned by corporations that our politicians past and present own privately for the most part.

The same was done in the 1980's when politicians came up with passing the laws required to start accredited on-line university's that are mostly the cause of our out of control student debt. This and the other self fulfilling legislation is what empties our government coffers and adds many zeros in their personal bank accounts.

The media of today gets the word out to the world today. Our countries dismal failures as well as the other countries failures are seen by the whole world now.

We all should know by now how bad the 1930's depression era by the stories our parents or grand parents would attest too. That depression too, also had direct involvement of Wall Street.

The American dream is fading in recent years for most people. This directly related new laws and deregulation of laws that were put there for a reason. The reason for such laws was for exactly to keep what is happening today from happening.

The companies that run themselves and make there own rules and regulating for themselves is the underlying problem. "We the people" now know definitely they are very greedy and run an auction for legal criminal activity that they still haven't received justice for. It is a known fact many of the same people involved in the 2008 meltdown are in high banking positions today.

Due to the GOP Tea Party and the pentagon war machine and the unnecessary and redundant trillions of dollars wasted in the almost decade lasting war we were dooped into.

This political theatre we are witnessing just to fill Dick and Bush Juniors and there cronies pockets. Not to forget the further filling of the pockets of the 1%. These created wars were the beginning of the downfall of this great countries great banking system and democracy itself.

Now we have to be aware of Liz Chaney and her democracy changing rederick foundation daddy's money started. That is trying to further her father's objective to ruin American democracy itself and blind to see it. This is GOP Tea Party trickle down economics 101 and we as a nation needs to make changes now today not in 2012 or beyond.

People in general are upset not only because of jobs disappearing out of our country due to bad and even premeditated self gratifying laws. Not to mention the sale of millions of shares of bottom Wall Street public junk that traded in the legal world wide scam that back fired.

Everybody's pension that did not cash in before the 2008 meltdown dropped in half its worth. As Dylan Ratigan says the things we need to debate now and fix now in our government. We need to overhaul our banking system. As we need to fix the problems in our education system from K- 12 and beyond. And most importantly "get the Money out of politics"

I am sure we are full of real life solutions and intelligent and common sense information. These books coming out like "those Greedy Bastards" as is this book. They are written to help get the word of the true democracy of America out!

I recall this is what the real America should and still should stand for still. Our proud citizens are very hungry to feel this love of our awesome country come together again. If we all work together we can and must accomplish true democracy strengthening. Something we as a county usually are associated with.

Chapter four

Moving up the ladder?

My parents were talked into having our family move to San Francisco, California in 1975 to open a Restaurant by and with my uncle Jack. This endeavor has changed the course of our family's closeness to this day. I was happy to leave that school and L.A. because of the abuse at school and I was also being abused by my brother's best friend. I was afraid to say anything because I was afraid of what might happen to me.

The S.F. area was a whole new experience in California and our politics. It was flower power V.W. bugs and vans for the then "Free Love and the peace" movement and live music in the golden gate park.

Streaking was all the rage back then. I was surrounded with a whole new world of music and hippies and I loved it. I remember in 1976 the fireworks show off floating barges on the bay celebrating the two hundred year birthday of the United States of America.

Now in 2012 our bay bridge in San Francisco 3000 plus jobs and bridge is made in China. The Iron that is used on the bridge is second rate melted down crap. The contracts were given to China too!! When are we going to wake up? Our government is bought at our current auction based government. O.K. I see we play by the rules while they manipulate there currency and trade!

We for instance pay 25% tariffs. They pay 2.5% is that fair? Also the excuse for us to accept their contract for building the bridge was it was cheaper! Well as it stands now not only did they not send enough steel they are charging us more unseen items and for the delays that they themselves created.

The SF-Bay Bridge is ending up costing us much more than the Bechtel Corporation would have charged. Also it would have been built completely by Americans but it would have built with our superior American iron.

Our family moved to the San Francisco bay area to see if we could achieve a few more notches up the ladder of success. We as a family all worked in and opened one of the first of Portuguese restaurants in the U.S.

We named it "A Bit of Portugal" it lasted about eight years and was located in El Cerrito, California. It had critical acclaim and came highly recommended by the famous San Francisco bay area restaurant guide writer and restaurateur Jack London.

My parents were always working 12+hours a day. I was going home to an empty house some thing I was not used to before our restaurant. After several years we sold it to the car dealership next door for a new showroom.

The people and the children were a little different minded in northern California then they were in Los Angeles. This was a culture shock for all five of us children. We were use to going to the beach often among other LA oriented things to do.

My middle sister Anna Bella was a track star at San Pedro high school and hated being uprooted from her popularity and friends to a whole new school and five hundred miles away from her friends.

So she ended up running away at 17 and went back to L.A. She got pregnant with her high school boyfriend and got married and never finished high school. Anna was married twice and has four beautiful kids.

All her kids remain in San Pedro except one in Oregon. Anna's first child Nicole just received her Masters Degree and has a good job but can't seem to land a job in her field of study.

Now my sister Anna is single again and living with her son, his wife and two children due to the economy. This is not due to the unwillingness of GOP bootstrap pulling garbage.

This is the outcome of our bought one sided Jaded greedy and the Wall Street barons. Not to mention the — Big Bank self lobbied laws for the rich only. And the new laws government enforce on there behalf we have bankrupting this country today! This economy and government structure if not fixed will be the demise of this country and current superpower. I call home.

If money was taken out of the equation, there would be much less if no corrupt career politicians. They just kick the can down the road if anything. Voters put theses people in office to do the necessary changes needed to run a great democracy.

The current truth is only if your community or state is lucky you will get one or two things done but the underlying problem is still not dealt with completely. Or if legislation can pass a new law to fix even a huge problem like the re- implementation of Glass – Steagle. It s was the law that regulated Wall Street and the banks after the great depression.

At the time my family moved to San Francisco I had just end of 5th grade at Elisabeth Stewart School. The teachers here were great. Then after that summer working at the restaurant, I started Jr. High School at Juan Crespi Jr. high School in El Sobrante, California.

I remember it was the time all of us students had to start getting used to undressing and showering in front of and with other students our own age. These and other new experiences that was pivotal in the future school experience for all students.

I remember kids were into experimenting with many different things like cigarettes, drinking and sex. My middle sister Alice got into the wrong crowd at Juan Crespi Jr High and ran away like my other sister Anna.

Alice did it Just to move into Pac Rats house with three other runaways. It was only when I started Jr high school in September many students knew of my sisters where abouts. It was directly across the street from my new Jr High school.

I went there to that house and talked her into coming back home until she eventually left for good at the age of seventeen. This practice was popular with the young Ladies with boy friends in school back then.

My parents started to need extra help at the restaurant so I found myself going to our restaurant a lot after school. I finished the eighth grade and started helping out at the restaurant that summer too.

I partially blame the schools for big drop out rates of the horrible broken public education system of the 1960's to today including my own.

Everyone that went thru a public education system knows that it is broken. This is especially true in poverty stricken areas. Preferential treatment, profiling and other discriminatory acts, by a growing percentage of horrible teachers and administrations with no morals.

I was also was experimenting with the popular San Francisco music scene back then. I ended up working for General Hee one of the "Flying Tigers" in Pinole, California. He was a great fighter pilot, boss and friend. I would go to the horse races with plenty cash and a list of horses he picked I remember he loved to gamble that's for sure.

Mr. Hee would sometimes give me a paid day off and send me to Golden Gate Field's raceway in Emeryville, California. This horse racetrack is built on the edge of the east bay. He won a lot of money and lost a lot too! He is a great man and he was a risk adverse person as I became.

He thought me a lot about respect, compassion and self constraint too recklessness. I learned some Chinese and cultural habits working for his loving family. I will never forget that man or what he showed and taught me. Over the two years I worked for him and his beautiful wife Lily it was very hard at times and great and fun others.

The Hee's like my parents loved this country and what it stands for "Mr. Hee actually killed in combat for our democracy". They worked very hard also and had a great middle class life. They all Enjoyed paying taxes and being a contributing members of the U.S. society. The U.S. still enjoys the least amount of personal taxes and consumer product taxes in the world.

For the summer of 1981 at age16, I went to work for a carpet, linoleum and tile showroom and installation business. The neighbor across the street from us in Pinole, California needed a helper and gave me the job one summer.

I was still a young republican back then, in fact one of my best friends father was the fire chief and one of the best lobbyists in the bay area. Then I worked with Dan at Pete Shoebers restaurant for a famous local athlete in Pinole.

Dan and I worked there and we lived in a Victorian in old town Pinole over the liquor store "it was both of ours very first apartment." We used to drink allot back then and love to cruise around. Dan and his new 22 shotgun got us in trouble.

I was going home once I knew he had the gun in a bag. I told him my father would kick me out of the house. That's exactly what happened after got us arrested for the first time by shooting out a light post in a stadium.

With a gun he got for hunting. What an idiot, I stopped hanging around him after that because he moved down to San Diego to work.

Paul's father still has influence in bay area politics today. Paul calls me a bleeding hart liberal these days. Paul, Dan and other friends from school also dropped out of high School to work for money.

Paul and I decided to get our general education diploma "GED" together and go to work fulltime. Work was easier to get then and was more than plentiful and people paid after the job was completed as normal.

One of the summer jobs I had growing up turned into an artistic love. I started A-1 tile & Design Tile received my contractor's license by the state of California in 1987. It was a great contracting business for me at the time. I had a great life back then until the economy died in 2007. Unfortunately I lost my father my business and everything I owned also later that year.

Paul was spending a lot of time on the family Christmas tree farm back East. When he could, I would put him to work when he came back to California. He then went back to University of Virginia where he received his bachelors in business.

As I said in 1987 I became licensed as A-1 Tile and started my business in Bell Marin Keys, California. I remodeled bathrooms and kitchens. I did work for some famous people as Anita Kornfeld and other great and very important people.

I continued working in Marin for many years in I lived in Mill Valley and then Sausalito, California. I had also met friends on jobs. I met this one nice guy and his name was Dan also. His brother had built a home made plane with a few of the rich neighborhood kids in the garage of the house I lived in for three years. It was on Dunfries Terrace in San Rafael.

I had a kitchen fire in mill valley and was looking for a new house to move too. Dan found out about it thru Joe a mutual friend. I got a call and met him out at the big empty house with an awesome three bridges, boat harbor and bay view on Dunfries Terrace.

The house was never touched since they had it built and it in the 1950's and it looked that way. Dan's brother was an airplane mechanic and built his own plane in the garage. He had been building a boat in the back yard also; it was never finished and still sitting in the back yard. I should have known then I was getting in over my head, but I liked Dan and the house and the location and I needed to move.

I loved living in that house, besides if I did not move in fast the homeowners insurance for that house would have been raised from several hundred a year to thousands of dollars that none of the brothers had. So I moved in and it solved both our problems.

I paid $300.00 a month and other bills a great deal for a 3200 square ft home to my self "even though it was a real dump" But it had a million dollar view!

Dan had three other older brothers and one sister who drowned in the back yard pool when she was very young. "I later found out" and I eventfully met them all. He had a very sad but rich upbringing.

His father was a war veteran and became hospitalized and died in the Napa state hospital and the hospital put a lien on his house on Dunfries Terrace for $270.000 and the houses in the neighborhood the were about $700.000 at the time.

Dan was going thru a separation of a long time girl friend. So Dan eventually moved in too. One night after dinner Dan and I came up with a plan to remodel and sell the house to pay off the hospital and government lien on his inheritance.

We both noticed that it was a government ploy for big money because they knew of his paid off San Rafael house and it worked! He was a veteran and should have been in a veteran's facility "no excuses" and they just got tired of fighting them in court and ended up paying 300K unfairly!

I worked very hard as did the brothers on that house. I had a verbal agreement and was told several times I was going to get paid $5,000 in the end. After we finish and sell the house. I was living there under all that demolition and remodeling.

A totally fair deal I thought for turning a half bath to a full bath all by myself, new plumbing included also a 6 foot Jacuzzi in the master bath with separate custom marble and glass block shower stall . A hallway full bath new tub toilet everything updated and new.

I also completely remodeled the laundry room. The huge kitchen tile floor and five granite countertops also the gorgeous marble entry way and a matching fire place and mantle. Oh and a half a Mercedes that I actually paid half for; apparently they never intended to pay me, as I never seen a penny to this day! And they sold that house for $550,000.

Actually I worked for Tracy a real nice lady three houses up the same street. We ran into each other as I was washing my truck on my driveway. She asked me over to do another job for her, this time her entry way.

I came by a few days later and gave her an estimate and she agreed to start the following week. It was the easiest commute I ever had. The day I was finished and we talked about me helping the brothers with the huge remodeling undertaking and selling of the house.

She also said to me how sad it was for everybody involved. I said yeah the dad dieing with that big unjust lien against the house. She said "I was talking about the Neighbor's sons." Sons I said "We were on her front steps as she was pointing to three separate houses on our street."

"Their son died" and pointed to the house across the street and then there son died and there's did too. I started tearing up and asked her to tell me all she knew.

I told her they just told me about their very young sister. She died tragically in the back yard pool. Then Tracy told me the part of the neighbor's kids to build that old homemade plane he died in Clearlake California.

She filled in facts I had no idea of and frankly never thought of goggling until I was writing this very book in November 2011. What I did not know of the neighbors kids that Tracy did not tell me that afternoon.

I also started to recall events that happened to me while living there that I felt and seemed strange. One day as I was driving up our street, the neighbor would run and get there dog when I drove up my driveway at the time and I thought it was strange until I was told the whole story, not bit and pieces and I never asked.

"That one neighbor yelled across the street very loudly! "Tragedy, Tragedy, Tragedy" then going back into her very nice home. The house was finished and I stared to look for a new home to live in.

I bought my very first home through the V.A list and moved to Fresno, California with my hard earned income. I wanted and needed my money and told them that more than once. What I thought was a good friend, Che called up Dan to tell them that I was going there to repossess the Mercedes!" I just needed the car or money soon.

As it turned out we Dan and I stated an export company also that did not workout even after a three week European sales trip we both took for Craig my other friend. We bought a Mercedes Benz 240 d together.

Che called Dan and I was ambushed at the front door. The realtor that worked for Anita Kornfeld called the police. On my expected visit by them, and I was arrested for using the fence for a weapon. "The fence they threw me against" not to mention my brand new truck.

My brand new truck door was damaged with my head two against one. I remember when the police asked for my ID the address on my drivers license was the same Dunfries address we were standing in front of.

The same address I lived at for three years not to mention remodeling it all. They should have been honest with me from the start and say you are working for free because the realtor I got them only could get an offer after a year on the market for 95 thousand less then what they wanted. They still pocketed over $265,000

They should have said we just want free work because you got to stay here or something! That mentality was the same at Jon's future job was identical. As my father and Paul both said to me "I should never combine business with friendships." What crap I thought.

I never saw my money or the Lacey's again. It was all about the money. It always seems to end that way.

"The Lacey incident was my second arrest!" many years ago!

The marin DA charged me with assalt with a deadly weapon; but the weapon was used on me along with my truck door with my head. "The fence" Greg and Dan just did not want to pay me. What they promised to pay for remodeling the big house. They lied to me like they did about the neighbor kids dieing in the plane with doug that sad day. Not to mention losing the Mercedes I paid half for? Paul and my father also told me I am to nice to people and they take advantage when they picked me up from jail!

6 Bodies Recovered From Plane That Crashed in Lake

October 01, 1990 | LOUIS SAHAGUN | TIMES STAFF WRITER

Divers removed six bodies from the wreckage of a World War II-era Navy patrol

plane that nose-dived into a Northern California lake after performing a impromto acrabatic monover. seaplanes, authorities said Sunday.

Federal investigators identified Santa Rosa airplane mechanic Doug Lacey as the pilot and owner of the twin-engine Lockheed P2V Harpoon that "buzzed" the crowd before slamming into shallow water at the western end of Clear Lake.

12:29 p.m. Saturday

There were no survivors aboard the plane.

The names of the five other victims were withheld pending notification of relatives. On Sunday, divers continued their search for a possible seventh victim although authorities doubted earlier reports that there were six passengers with Lacey.

A large crane was used to haul out pieces of the plane's engines, hull and wings, authorities said.

Lacey, who took off Saturday from Sonoma County Airport, was apparently trying to impress friends at the seaplane convention when his bulky aircraft plunged into six feet of murky water and silt about 50 yards offshore.

"He came to buzz the hell out of a few friends at low altitude and then get out," said a federal investigator who asked that his name not be used. "He got carried away. It was really stupid."Witnesses said Lacey made several low passes over stunned spectators onshore and floating seaplanes meeting in the lake for the 11th annual "Seaplane Fly-In" organized by the Seaplane Pilots Assn.

The plane's last maneuver was similar to a barrel roll.

"He kept going up until he lost flying speed, stalled, rolled over and went down," said Stan Sinn, a witness and spokesman for the pilots'association. "That thing went straight in and disintegrated in one big splash."Sinn said organizers of the convention had planned to report the "uninvited and unwanted" plane, even before it crashed into the lake about 100 miles north of San Francisco.

"Even if he hadn't crashed, we were going to report him to the Federal Aviation

Administration," Sinn said. "If the guy wanted to kill himself, he shouldn't have solicited a bunch of people to go down with him."

CHAPTER FIVE
Dreaming with ventures

It all started with a trip to the Lacey family grave site. It felt strange being asked to go at first, but at that time my friendship with Dan Lacey and his brothers was very strong. I thought it was besides they really wanted me to go with them because of all my help beyond the big remodeling job.

We got to the cemetery and they were looking around for there parents and sister's grave sites. They kept walking back and forth when I finally said "what in the heck are you doing?" They said "its close we will find them" "What?" I said. Well they kept saying "we think there right here" and "They don't have head stones."

Watching grown men cry was sad for me in many ways. Lately I have been coming to grips why Dan kept the whole truth from me and Anita. Now that I lost my brother tragically too I seem to understand better. All those sad looks I got from the neighbors all makes sense to me now. Like when I was home washing my car or watering the lawn or gardening, it was the parents that lost there sons.

I asked Che if she can help me get head stones made for them and she and I arranged to have them made in at the piedmont mortuary. I then went to the Lacey grave site and asked to have the newly surveyed cemetery plots of the actual lacey grave sites.

When the head stones were ready, I took the older Lacey with me and on the way to the cemetery I told him what we were going to do. I wanted it to be as a surprise Dan and Greg also. I mixed some mortar and installed all three headstones with Dan and Greg's brother.

The remodeling and then selling of the house, that was a plan we had come up with using Anita my confidant and muse and vice versa "at the time." And she and I both eventually saved "those Lacey boys" as Anita called them lovingly.

First we had to get all the brothers to agree on the new plan. I got Anita Kornfeld the listing and she referred her super cool loan officer to help with the financing for Dan and Greg. First thing was to pay off the government lien and pay for the materials ECT. For the remodel, the loan was costly though. If I new before they signed I would have talked them out of it.

Anita sold the hard to sell house for $550,000. I did not see a dime after the sale. I was even arrested for trying to get my car back.

Dan Lacey and I started Gate Five Exports together for our "Christmas saver invention." Together and Dan helped me with my own Platapussy's invention, also with the help from David the Patient attorney in San Francisco, California.

"I believe my idea was stolen, my invention that is currently being sold today" yet another big hardship that happened. I am still in the understanding and amazement mode how he could get away with it to this day. I put so much time, money and effort into the invention only to have my patent lawyer tell me "it's a sex toy, you can't get a patent on that!" well it s being in many sex oriented magazines.

So I let Dan get into my other new venture with Craig a friend of mine who made great living selling large amounts of steel to the Japanese. One day he asked me to go to his country club with him for a swim and a workout. After the work out we went to Rancho Liquors for some cold drinks.

He went on telling me about how bad he was doing. He also thinks "due to the Japanese buying recycled steel. He might reach some very tough times ahead .I had a great idea!! I heard that the Japanese love California wine they would bring back after sending sake here.

"Sell them wine from California I said." The label we eventually created from my idea. "California Gold Cellars" Craig went full steam ahead with my idea and he made Dan and I head of sales in Europe at my request. Craig already had a letter of credit and the means and ways to get it there.

Craig came by Dunfries and picked us up in his silver BMW Convertible with the top down. Then we drove up Highway 101 north to Sonoma County. As we were driving up north I was planning a European sales trip.

It was a very nice trip that day. We got to taste all the different wines they had to offer. We all gave input to pick out wine mixture formulas for our own label of wine. We came up with "California Gold Cellars."

Craig made a bundle on my idea "even won a prestigious award in Osaka Japan." Dan and I talked him into expanding to Europe that day. We started off in England where they now sell a lot of our wine.

They laughed at us! Saying "we have French wine" t was no laughing mater for us, we were spending a lot of cash. I remember it was a hot July and we had suits on carrying heavy wine in a cooler.

Well we were ahead of our time because California wine is sold in huge quantities in England nowadays. We had a blast running around Europe trying to sell the wine. To be completely honest when we got to France we got tired of being laughed at!! I will never forget that trip.

After Dan and I went to France we stopped trying to sell the wine and stated drinking it ourselves. Frankly we all knew at that point it was too soon for our idea to take hold in the euro zone.

We also went to see Danielle a French woman who purchased John and Anita Kornfeld's gorgeous Lucas valley home. I remodeled that Ikelier designed home some for Anita and John and Some for Danielle.

My dear friend Anita Kornfeld wrote "The Vintage" It was on the best seller list for weeks and "In a Blue Birds' eye." The vintage was then made into the T.V. mini series Falcon crest. There was some controversy over the particular creative problem was settled.

Anita just recently retired from real estate and is now writing a new book. I feel it is going to be her best yet. She read a little to me over the phone recently and it's a big hit. It should be coming out soon. Her daughter is an accomplished writer also. Marsha wrote a children's book and illustrated it with her own superbly tasteful art.

There was a second career Anita loved, real estate and she was very successful at it. That is how I met her one nice spring day in 1987. John her loving husband called me to there Lucas Valley home at the time for an estimate on remodeling a bathroom.

Not to long after that they sold the house to Danielle who I love dearly also and ended up doing much more work at now Danielle's home. She sold high end art at a gallery in Marin County California.

She had me do her kitchen at her new home then she sold it. She had fallen in love with a married man on a trip to France to see her mother. Soon after that she sold the house and moved to Gronoble France to live. That great lunch at the square with Dan was the last time I saw her.

Dan Lacey and I had bought a car in Holland because it was much cheaper than renting for weeks. The remaining cases of wine were getting to be hard to lug around on the trains. That was an experience in itself and was a big factor to buying a car.

We were going to rent a car until we found out it was going to cost $2,300.First Dan started calling the car adds from the local Rotterdam classifieds and most people did not speak English that answered for him.

I am laughing now as I was then. Let's just say none of that part of the trip was easy. I came up with what turned out to be a good idea we went to the nearest bar and had the English speaking barman to call the car adds. Then he had them drive the cars to the bar for us to look at them.

After a few clunkers showed up this man that owned a local dealership sold us a Peugeot station wagon. It was a trade in he sold us for $750 dollars. Jorgen was his name; he was a great and very honest car man. Once he knew we were going to drive to France then Italy then to Spain & Portugal, he had his mechanic go over it. We picked up the car at his dealership the next day and headed straight to France.

When we got to Gronoble our car was broken into in the middle of town at noon. We were having lunch with Danielle it was a very fun day until we got back to the car. We did not want to spend money on auto glass. So we decided to stop hauling all our wine and started drinking it and giving it away as tips.

We also decided to go straight to Portugal. We had a great time I am sure we will never forget that summer. When we got back to Marin the house was getting sold so the brothers and I had to find new places to live. I ended up getting a house on a Veterans Administration list for homes. I bought a large home in Fresno, California.

Greg and Dan both bought houses in Marin. Dan in Corte Madera I believe San Rafael for Greg. Got to admit it took a couple years to forget that huge stab in the back from the Lacey's both and Che both. I am so nice people think I will work for free? I still have a big problem with that. Is that why the cliché "nice guys finish last" Dang it!

I thought they were good friends too especially after helping them through the mess left for them to deal with. No words to describe how sorry for his and the neighbors losses but I write this in memory of the lacey family and the neighbors sons.

Anita at the time thought if the house was empty it would sale faster? I new better, even then it sounded hinky. Nowadays they have to stage an expensive house to even sale it. And believe me the house was boastfully beautiful when done.

Anita to this day did not know about the neighbors sons either. I will let her read the rest of my book soon. She will put it all together as I recently did. It felt as something was the mater as the months went by. The views were of the San Rafael Bridge and on a nice day you can see all the way to the top of the golden gate bridge & "Mount Tam" also knows to the locals as the breast of a beautiful naked lady lying down.

CHAPTER 6

Must start a new career

Paul and a couple others from our old Juan Crespi school days decided to go back to school to achieve a higher Education. Dan my childhood friend moved away to San Diego to work on a fishing boat and live with his ex step mom Ava and his new lover.

"Wow" Dan got his step mom pregnant as did his father and she had both their kids. Paul spilled that on me before one year when he went back east to the University of Virginia to achieve his dream. Paul achieved his degree in business at University of Virginia in a few years. I never saw neither Dan again to this day.

Everyone is very proud of Paul and what he accomplished with his life. By continuing with school and getting a useful degree he now works for a major investment banking firm earning over six figures a year.

That accomplishment made me dream to get a degree of my own. I had to do something anyhow because the economy got me hard. So I started planning a school endeavors went to Williamsville, New York to start my educational venture. The school Emily Dickinson went too.

Paul and his degree made it to a major league manager director of a big investment bankers firm. My childhood friend Paul has made and worked his way ground up that currently fading ladder to success.

Paul you see is now part of the 1% population. Paul reached his dream of being as he puts it "In the lucky sperm club" The one percent. It just made it much more of an incentive for a degree especially after the economy went south and in my field.

I love both him and his wife of 17 years Teresa. I also loved staying over at there house, as a guest in there mini mansion many nights. I even truly enjoyed staying at there old smaller house too.

This whole Che deal has me still trying to figure out what exactly happened to our relationship. I feel that they think I am jealous of there self made situation I suppose. Che lives in a three million dollar house that I remodeled for next to nothing also.

My father told me before he died recently "in this world you have to very careful who you trust."The problem is I never was or am now jealous of any of my rich friends. I really can't understand why some people can't just enjoy life without creating more drama.

The problem is when we all moved back to the bay area recently I introduced them to Che. Wow when Che got herself involved yet again something happened. So I ended all those big old drama filled friendships of many years that only caused me many problems I never wanted.

Never once did I get the feeling of jealousy from Paul and me for him. I believe it is that feeling of having a great lifestyle again that sparked me. Because when I lived and worked in Marin he would enjoy a few different homes of I lived in. I believe as I did some of the clients I worked for.

Things like ocean views witch he finally has now and much more. The reason I am explaining this part of my life and Paul's is that it seemed to be a pivotal choice to go back to school to get a degree. For Paul and a lucky one, close to fifty percent of university graduates obtain a good job after obtaining a degree in there field of study.

Paul went full throttle for a degree at a higher educational institution after community college. I never asked him, but we know each other enough. I still believe it was to show his father and me, he was smart enough he could pull it off. I knew he could do it right away, once he told me part of his plan.

Well now I am all alone and just call my 85 year old mother in Portugal. You know she keeps asking me when I am going to finish university and get a degree. I haven't told her yet, In order to finish school now.

I have to move out of state to do that because of the unfair and morals-less Tea Party University ruling. The plan to go back to school for Paul to get a degree certainly paid off for Paul.

That University degree helped propel him to move up that more illusive ladder to success and the American dream. He even parleyed his degree and made it to the 1% of real life dreamers that actually made it.

The lifestyle in Marin and that type of life seems to be over for me in the last several years. My hard work and nice lifestyle in Marin is partially what made Paul want to go back to school and frankly me too. I am quiet sure he aimed for that 1% and I am very proud of him and what he achieved.

One day years ago, he was dropping me off at the Louisville airport and I told him I was very proud of him. Sometimes I wonder if he knew what I meant. I can only hope he wants the same for me again I hope?

Well Paul loaned me a chunk of my down payment on this house I am living in now. That action said to me that he is still my best friend. That was one more reason for me to go back to school for a higher education.

Another was unfortunately do to the economy I really did not have a choice. The housing market and banking system collapsed completely in 2008. People stopped remodeling to there homes, adding on too or even paying for work performed.

Most people became upside down in there mortgages also. That's how I eventually lost it all and became homeless after more than twenty years hard work. Flat broke and nothing more than the clothing I had on at the time and the stuff Paul had saved for me.

Well on my brother Joe and his girlfriend's engagement anniversary. He took the day off but they called him in anyway. That day he did not have to take Michael their son to day care "the only good thing about that day." He was called in to work for a last minute fill in.

He got onto the interstate 80 freeway headed toward Vallejo, California. There is a big hill that crests at the last rest area before getting into the San Francisco's bay area where he worked.

That day a driver decided to get off at the Highway 37 exit just over that hill. The problem was she was on the fast lane and caused a twenty some odd car pile up. Out of all the broken arms, legs and other injuries my brother was the only one who died.

A part of me died that day also and I still grief of that day all these years later. His death made me want to live life to the fullest. I still think of him a lot especially when I get in a bind. I do really miss him.

My sister Alice told the family that he was unhappy with is life and "he wanted to die." She said they were swinging his son with her in the hallway at the hospital waiting for my dad. I normally don't believe her but this time I did for some reason she has a way with telling people things bluntly. From that day on I looked at my life differently. Life is more fragile and more real to me lately.

With the many trips I took to Portugal to be with my ageing parents. I found myself loving living in Parents birthplace myself. During one of my visits I was lucky enough to get in the film industry while visiting.

My first job was audience enthusiasm for 17 shows. You can see them on you tube under "Malta Gira" RTP1 they have millions of views. That job turned into a few successful castings. Then a Principal acting job in a huge promo for the Portuguese tourism board and was on CNN international in 1998.

The Cleo award winner was an ICEP commercial for the Portuguese tourism board. Being the principal actor in it and it won a Cleo award later that year. I also was a principal actor in over ten other well know commercials and other film work.

My friend in Portugal got a gig in a house band on a Varity show. He got me a ticket and my acting career started completely by incidents and luck I suppose. The variety show was a funny stupid human tricks type game show. I was laughing so loud they gave me a job.

Then I did a casting and nailed it, then a couple of spots on different soap operas. A cameo on a music video played on MTV and VH1 for Caroline Records in New York. I also loved my parts on a sitcom and a very popular live broadcasted variety show. I remember both shows made me not be able to take public transit without being pointed at!

Believe me it was my live show work and movie parts that I loved doing the most. I just like entertaining as a new form of expression. I found it by accident and it is fun for me even with the very long hours involved in doing a great job at it. I made some pretty good money also.

During that time, I had the pleasure to work on the same show as Cher. She was in Portugal on her huge "Believe" album tour. I also worked on a variety show with Ricky Martin on his "shake it up" tour in Portugal.

Not to mention being in a critically acclaimed Portuguese movie with Joaquin de Almeida called "Tentaciao." I also had several speaking parts in a French movie called "Baldie" with Charles Aznavour in Portugal. I loved being in the entertainment industry in Portugal so much when I went back home I moved back to L.A. to get it a try.

I recall walking on the private beach at paradise cove in Malibu where I ended up living. One night I remember walking across the street, "where they used to film the Rockford files" it was where Jimbo lived at in the TV show.

Two identical curly white little poodle type dogs, they belonged to James Brolin and Barbara Strisand who live on the cliff nearby? They came to me while on the private beach and sniffed me out. They sat down and kicked back with me as I drank a beer at the edge of the surf.

I moved into Cindy's huge Condo on the land side of P.C.H. as she and the other owners were fighting their HOA for some work that needed to be done on the Malibu condo complex.

Her friend was the "little house on the Prairie's" real life mother of the little girl. Who I found out was one of two identical twins that shared a part in the famous TV series. She looked identical to Susanne Summers and was a great friend and neighbor.

She would get mixed up by the paparazzi who still hang out at the Starbucks in Malibu. They still live on the same stretch of Pacific Coast Highway so it was easy for the mix up.

Its funny, if you were to put the two in the same room you would think they were actual twins. They also live only a few blocks away one another one on the beach and the other on the land side of PCH.

One day doing an errand for my ex roommate, she asked me to go to Santa Monica, California to get her prescriptions for her broken leg. While there I went to the MGM offices on the way home.

I was in the copy room downstairs working on my face shot. This turned into what I thought was a lucky break at the time. I then went to Mary Jo Slater's office she is Christian Slater's mother who had an office there. It so happened to be upstairs from the copy room at MGM. I was lucky enough to look like the deaf Marks Brother.

Her office sent me to Dream Works for an interview that same day. I was sent there for a casting to be one of the Marks Brothers in a film about them that I believe never got made. I also was feeling guilty not getting home faster with her pills.

When I got home she was upset. She used the fact that the over thirty bottles of wine and spirits that I just unloaded on the garage floor. "I just bought out the liquor store of all its 50% off sale wine and some bottles of spirits at the local store.

Her F.B.I. boss came to pick up her cruiser and noticed all that liquor. I have to admit it did look like we were a couple of lushes. She used that embarrassing situation I put her in as an excuse for us to part ways. The truth is I seem to love to purchase bargains and shop that way to this day.

Well I moved to Palm Desert and so I decided it was time for me to get started on my higher education. Anita Kornfeld my Marin client and friend helped me find a very nice condo overlooking the Palm desert Valley, below Buckhorn.

So I purchased that beautiful condo then started school at the College of the Desert down highway 74 in February 2000 in Palm Desert, California. I felt proud of my 3.30 GPA two semesters running.

At that point it was over 20 years before I returned to educate myself further in school. I was awarded that year with a Mary Bono scholarship. I was happier with life back then. The problem with the beautiful desert is the summer months were getting intolerable for me.

On a summer desert escape vacation to Toronto to visit my friends from Portugal I fell in love. At least once in our life we should be so lucky to have a true love affair. Oh well that relationship ended up as a huge real life learning situation as well. I sold everything in palm desert and moved to Niagara Falls.

That's when I went to the nearby famous writer Emily Dickinson's School at Erie Community College in Williamsville, New York. I took her same English Lititutre class with a 3.0 GPA. This is where I began my writing of poetry.

Yes I was in Niagara Falls on 911 and witnessed first hand hundreds of cars and people not able to cross the U.S. and Canadian border and stuck on both sides for miles.

A lot of them were stuck without the money or able to go to work or back home for days. The days that they were blocked from crossing until the U.S. government felt what it needed to do next. Cars were stuck from the bridges and back for miles. Some people were so nice to let some of these people stay and eat at there homes.

Yes I did see and feel the fear in the air first hand. I was not at ground zero but I did experience 911 at a nearby New York border town. I will never forget 911; it was the same day I realized I fell in love with a true to life gold digger.

That September 9th I threw a big birthday bash for the gold digger I loved with all my hart. I moved back east from California for a real life love story I thought! It was all one big well thought out manipulation. I was blind and not seeing the manipulation at first. Niagara Falls, also a town of love, honeymoons and marriages, and one of the big wonders of the world.

We had a new venture to start we were going to open a new nightclub party spot with live music and DJ nights. After losing the financing for the club and my relationship I was heartbroken. A lot of hard work and most of my life's resources were depilated again at that point.

Knowing I really was a true Californian and was already tired of shoveling snow so off I was again. My sister Alice had money she said she would loan me but changed her mind and stopped talking to me until she was out of money again many years later herself.

So I moved to Miami, Florida in 2003 and continued my higher education at Miami Dade College. I took broadcasting and went to Telemondo studios where they film Sabado Gigante and the Cristina show. "My mother's favorite shows when she lived in u.s."

For school I rented this apartment from a crazy Cuban lady that was married to a realtor. She new I was a Contractor before going to College and called me daily with a problem in one of the many units.

The problem was she did not pay enough for the nuisance calls. I got tired of being bothered by the fast load of crap I was talking from that crazy Cuban. I was being railroaded again. So I moved again.

Because I am nice to people "My father and Paul reminded me of this more than once" people think because I am nice they think I like working for free?" Who in this world does unless agreed too in the beginning or dose it on one's free will?

I do like Florida but did not like the weather much it rained too much and was too muggy for me. I then moved back to Monterey, California. I got this roommate in Pacific Grove, California. I lived there with a "three dog night" member's stepson. I ended up going back to College in Salinas and its famous Theatre dept.

My roommate took me to Monterey bar on New Years Eve. Where I met another big love of my life in that lasted a few years but was also a mistake because of an age gap and another DJ dream again.

Then I went back to Marin fulltime to return to what I thought where I left off but the best of housing market was nearing its run. The fraud closure foreclosures were starting to take place.

In the big way I was the major grief and worry. 2007 I experienced the loss of my father. Also my mothers fell and broke her hip at the age of 80. It happened one day after my father's funeral. I had to double back to Portugal from home in California.

Coming back to Marin was sad and when I got back the economy was worse than when I had left. I had put everything I own tools electronics antiques, clothing, some gold jewelry and art. I already experience the loss of my large home.

Most everything I had left was gone now. It was all gone because of an error by Bank of America Credit Card Company. It was a twenty dollar mistake that was paid late! "If I had left it all at Paul's Kentucky house where I just brought it from I would still own it all."

By the time I got back to U.S. the storage company had already auctioned off over $36,000 in years of hard work for $300.00. I was never notified due to being out of the country. "they could have e-mailed me" Even though the manager promised to me I had nothing to worry about as I told him I needed to go take care of my mom.

I even put a second case hardened master lock on the storage unit before going to help my Mother in Portugal. Horrified is the feeling and still remember that feeling of being completely destroyed again for trusting people.

I found myself camping around and couch hoping at friend's homes. I was Devastated again for weeks and stayed at a Ray's cabin in Washington, California. I finally was coming to grips of the major grief I still have do to loosing all my worldly possessions.

My father passed away April, 1st. 2007 and my mother needed me so I headed back to Portugal. My then 82 year old mother needed with everything at that time to fulfill my father's last wishes and help out my mom who fell and broke hip the day after my dad's funeral.

I lost all my documents my contractors license, passport, birth certificate, G.E. Diploma, SS card, and the deed to Lake Arrowhead lot and other very important documents, Jewelry, coin collection, electronics, Art

Everything! It was very hard dealing with daily life needing something you don't have anymore. You learn to make do with less. Making a full list of items lost and then I began realizing and remembering buying a lot in Lake Arrowhead many years ago to build a vacation home.

So I moved down to L.A. again and went to San Bernardino College in 2007 with a 3.0 GPA. I was able to sell the lot in Lake Arrowhead to my neighbor in 2008.

I moved back up to northern California where I lived in Ray's Cabin up by Grass Valley, California for five months while looking for a home to buy. I ended up finding a small house that was affordable in Oak Park, Sacramento where Kevin Johnson our current mayor is from he is "the ex boyfriend of Michelle Kwee" somebody that proved that we can overhaul this educational system. Michelle Kwee was making great strides in Washington D.C...

The problem with that is the people in charge could not get away with bad administrations, corruption and the continued wasteful and useless spending of dollars as the CSU, and others demonstrated. So the polarities and Randi Wingarten of the American Federation of Bad tenured teachers and a million extra dollars spent on an election that ended our education problem's fixer career.

The fact that I needed to find a new career was clearly evident too. Due to the economy I needed to get a degree in something useful that can help me get a good job. So I got focused on achieving my degree and found Sac State to be a good starting point. "So I thought"

I used the lake lot sale money and some I borrowed from Paul to fix the neglected and vandalized home I have now. I purchased my house in Sacramento on my birthday December 3rd 2009 and just finished it recently.

This house is located in a neighborhood that people were shot, burglaries and drive by shootings all in the last three years I lived here all on this block. Since the police have been here they stopped knocking on my door to try selling me things. So I usually don't even answer my door!

CHAPTER 7

Following the dream

My new home I worked so hard to get was in escrow and my new Sac State CSU University was five minutes away and starting in January 2009. The buying process of buying a home turned out to be a longer than normal.

This was caused by the mortgage and Bank mess of 2008 "it took over 90 days to close what was 30 days. It was only until February 20th 2009 to close. I also thought I was not going get the house and I already started at Sac State my new university. The house was empty and a big mess, while in escrow it was vandalized.

I was under huge stressing situations then, between the closing of escrow on my home. It was broken into once more during escrow. At that time the damage needed to be repaired right away or the escrow would fall out and lose the house.

The mandatory math class that I needed to complete within a year was stressful. I also was in the middle of moving into my new home. I pulled a mussel in my back moving a new mattress into the home I was moving into, all taking place in the middle of my first semester.

I saw the school counselor at Sac State and she knew I was dealing with many hardships all at once and the new stress of a big new school load. She suggested I see a school psychiatrist. I was told to join students with disability because I felt I was going to need some tutoring help for my mandatory CSU math requirement.

The school physiologist gives me ten packages of free trial Depacote. It made me feel absolutely terrible and made me tired all day. "I threw them away immediately"

I told him that the pills did not work for me and he gave me Ambian trial pills. They made me tired and lifeless so I decided that the docs are quacks and stopped seeing them but it was too late again.

This time I was labeled falsely and they decided to label me with manic depression anyway. "I thought what a load of crap." I go in with a mid life crisis "I lost my father then all of my worldly possessions and I became homeless for the first time in my life, also recently.

Maybe I am ADHD but certainly not manic. I am usually very happy in life and never had even entered my mind. One of my doctors or my friends and family would know something before age 45?

The school psychologist was supposed to offer the

Following=

To provide counseling, instruction, and mentoring for those struggling with social, emotional, and behavioral problems

To increase achievement by assessing barriers to learning and determining the best instructional strategies to improve learning

To promote wellness and resilience by reinforcing communication and social skills, problem solving, anger management, self-regulation, self-determination, and optimism

To enhance understanding and acceptance of diverse cultures and backgrounds

To collect and analyze data related to school improvement, student outcomes, and accountability requirements

To implement school-wide prevention programs that help maintain positive school climates conducive to learning

To promote school policies and practices that ensures the safety of all students by reducing school violence, bullying, and harassment

To respond to crises by providing leadership, direct services, and coordination with needed community services

To design, implement, and garner support for comprehensive school mental health programming

They did next to none of these for me; all they did was giving me pills! They did not help in any other way. If they had I would be graduating from CSU Sacramento State. The expensive semester wasted on a professor that spoke broken English.

He spoke with a very heavy accent witch made it very difficult to understand him at all. That made a hard course much harder and

The hard to understand professor made it extremely difficult to concentrate and grasp the subject that I already had a problem with. It came at a high cost of approx $5,000 a class. This made me more upset at the lack of help given after it was specifically asked for help in the sessions?

I ended up dropping math for a fresh start the next semester after summer break. Hopefully with a teacher that spoke clear English. The DRS issued me a new teacher and math tutor that next semester.

Well as fate had it, on July 1st, 2009. My car was stopped behind a few cars waiting for the cars before me to get on the freeway. When suddenly I was struck from behind so hard it knocked my whole body forward.

First my whole body twisted and flung into the steering wheel simultaneously hitting my head on rearview mirror and it came off. As my body twisted I felt a sharp pain in my back and neck was throbbing. The impacts also had me in shock and what seemed in full panic mode.

My left arm all the way up to my neck was numb and bleeding. Then the car struck again with a lesser impact and my car leached to the right when my body flew into the steering wheel and windshield again.

Thank god the air bag did not go of because I feel I would have been worse off like my brother. This all happened very fast then the man who hit me came to my window and asked if I was o.k. "I told him no." I was then asked by the SMUD security patrol to move the car across the street and he called the ambulance.

I was at the hospital laying on a gurney with major pain and they gave me a cat scan but not an MRI. I had even asked for one but the emergency room was overflowing in the hallways.

At that time a police officer came in emergency room and asked me if I was on a cell phone "I said no" then he asked me if I was stopped with a few cars ahead of my car. "I said yes"

As it turned out the driver of the car was Portuguese too and he thought he knew me from some restaurant he asked me about. That man and his wife left the scene of the accident as I was being wheeled away in an ambulance.

The very next day I could barely move and was in the worst pain in my life. It was like having the pain of two broken arms and legs at the same time; unrelenting even while trying to sleep.

I needed some pain relief but was terrified to drive but my pain was worse than my fear. I spent the following weeks at different doctors and not getting better at all.

First they sent me to a chiropractor he is a great guy but I was not getting better as much as I tried for weeks. I was told that my impact was a low speed impact with not much damage to my car. I told them it was my health that maters to me and I needed a doctor who can help.

They said to find a new lawyer and at that point I was happy to oblige. They were one of those ambulance chaser commercials I saw on local T.V. that night I was hit. I found a new lawyer and a new doctor and he finally said that I needed an MRI "something I asked for weeks" to get down to finding the root cause of my pain problem.

Over 12 months of different types of physical therapy the new doctor finally referred me to get a MRI. The therapy helped some with mobility but that did not help me and my major daily pain.

The MRI showed my neck problem and my major back problem. The MRI showed a torn spine and the need for a fusion operation. The spine trauma received also gave me Colitis something I thought I got from all the cheap fast food I ate while being mostly bedridden for months.

In the first grueling months of excruciating pain it was hard for me to move at all let alone stand and cook. I have been embarrassed, even though he did tell me to lose weight and stay away from fast food. He is a tall younger doctor with a caring touch and feel for his patients.

Now all I needed was a referral for the surgeon from my primary care physician. Getting the Insurance to do the surgery was the hardest hurdle to deal with. Especially with all the excruciating pain I was dealing with.

I have been dealing with major pain for over two and a half years now. It seems to be having a negative effect on my current regular health also. I just wanted my old life back! I truly wished I was never rear ended and injured this severely.

The end of August came and CSU Sacramento was starting again. The last semester I had a 3.30GPA. Due to my excruciating back pain received from that life changing horrible car accident.

I was not able to complete school due to not being able to sit or stand to long. I began to miss classes and ended up having to drop out of school as a result of my injury. So I dropped out of classes by putting the necessary form in the box by the counselor's office but they did not acknowledge it and my GPA dropped as a result.

The CSU's DRS office and the school psychologist should have did the there job and intervened. As I said they did not do a thing for my situation. So I called the dean and he said I was dropped and not return to Sac State.

He had a VERY bad attitude and I told him he was an over paid and useless dean. So he sent a university police officer over to my house. The officer tells me not to go to the school or I would be arrested! So I never went back!

I keep asking myself before this situation. Is it that I have stupid written on my face? Everyone that gets to know me understands that racism and discrimination is Key!

CHAPTER 8
HIGHER EDUCATION CORUPTION

On my birthday December 3rd 2010, I was admitted to CSU Stanislaus in Turlock, California. I was hospitalized again in January and missed some classes. I joined the DRS disability resource services headed by Lee Bettencourt.

Turns out he is another fellow Portuguese American that apparently bends over for his useless and over paid corrupt CSU title. The second time this CSU office did not help me as a paying student at all. In fact he gave out confidential doctor patent information from CSU Sac state reports to Denis, Shivani, Espinosa, Windy Smith and Brett Conner and others.

Lee Bettencourt and these other faculty and staff used Sac State reports against me to expel me as I will further explain.

You need to know why I picked and chose this school. This particular CSU has a Portuguese Cultural curriculum and it looked like a better school for me. I thought I would get a better education and fairness if I went to this school.

It is an hour and a half one way drive to get too. Also they would certainly understand my cultural traits for a good educational experience as they do for Hispanic community on campus.

The teacher had dropped me out of a few classes so I had to scramble to get others to fill the total of twelve units needed. I spoke to Dr Wang and she said I could not join her class. I then went to the dean's office and got help getting into what turned out to be Dr Wang's class after all.

I thought I was going to be happy that my math teacher Sheri Hoover. Well on my first day of school she handed me the class syllabus and straight out she said "good luck getting on the class website."

The problem with the teacher's discriminatory remarks was and became directly the start of a much bigger and costly problem for me the taxpayers.

The problem is that she said I was given the time I missed due to being hospitalized and sick. She said "I would be giving you preferential treatment" if she gave me the two weeks I missed. "Even though she said she did"

The work I fell behind were hundreds of problems to solve and 5 long tests. "In three days" I only had time to do about half and so I did what I could and she was failing me purposely anyhow. I knew I had no chance to pass with her. So I went to the math department head and we agreed for me to stop going to her classes.

I was to take the ELM test again or take the class again the next semester another $5,000 wasted. "I was used to knowing bad teachers again by now." They spend too much class time on there personal stories. Its o.k. if you're not paying thousands of dollars for a higher education.

One story in particular about her CSU math teaching husband having too many school loans and having to move to Turlock from Oregon. Another one about buying only clearance clothing and having a hard time paying back both of their current student loans.

Was this a story? Or was it her way to discourage us math challenged students in her remedial math class not go to school? "That's what it felt and sounded to me." I did think the story of her Irish College friend and their drunken Las Vegas trip. That's what I got out of those thousands of dollars for my mandatory math classes and $58,000 in school loans.

Later that week I received a school wide email that said Ricky Martin is dead! In bold type just like that. Well as fate had it I met and worked with him personally in Portugal "when he was on his shake t up tour. I was heartbroken to say the least and very sad that day.

The next day I received another email stating they had his name wrong. At that time, after being told by more than one student to be aware of the corrupt schools faculty and administration. I had then learned about the Sarah Palin CSU corruption debacle.

At that point after professor Hoovers blatant discriminatory remarks. This school was undeniably a Tea Party corrupt University. I was determined to get the best of my educational investments worth and get something out of my thousands of dollars spent there.

My history class at CSU Stanislaus with Dr Shue Wang's class started at 11 am ended at 12:30pm. My next Communications class was at 5pm the same days. The comm. 2000 class was instructed by Ashley Albertoni a very young and inexperienced teacher as most of the class agreed. I must add that Miss Hoover's class was in the very same classroom as Ashley Albertoni the very next period. One of my class mates heard them talking about me.

There was a school play that I really wanted to see that on may 5th at night. I had just finished driving the hour and half drive to school. At that time all the students in the classroom and I was waiting for Mrs. Albertoni for more than ten minutes. We students were just about ready to leave when she came rushing in late with a very bad attitude.

She also came to class wearing one skin tight see threw leotard with no undies on "you could see her everything." Finals were coming up and all I did was asking the questions the other students and I had been talking about while we were waiting for her to come teach the class.

Ashley then said as she pointed to me to "get out of classroom now and leave!" I was very upset at that point and said "I had not driven an hour and a half to be sent home for no good reason" Just for asking questions of our upcoming final? It certainly felt like she had planned the whole thing.

A fellow student in the comm2000 Class with Ashley named Heaven e-mailed me to file a complaint about her. I did just that to Denis V.P. faculty and staff. I e-mailed him on May 6th asking him to email all students and get the truth but he had another idea.

I was emailed not to go to the remainder of her classes and just so everybody knows. I was told by other students that she changed the final all together because of her not giving graded work so we can improve our final grade as I stated in my complaint.

She was preferential to her one on one teaching as she stated she was doing via email! She did not like my political speeches I wrote and let me know that. Ashley also told me they were opinions and not truth! All she needed to do is fact check!

All I wanted was a teacher in class to teach us while we are in class not just sitting in a corner having us read our speeches and imputing low grades on blackboard. By not giving us our graded past speeches until the last week of school, just how were we going to improve?

Every body was complaining about the final and that she did not give the corrected previous work turned in. This made it very hard to get a better grade since we could not see how she graded the work until the last week of school, when the teacher piled all our graded speeches all on her desk. My graded work was missing for some reason? This was supposed to be a University education not a high school type.

I complained to her that this was the reason to sign that yellow credit non credit slip she refused to sign. The class was my witness to this and her behavior to me that day also was clear. I spent all four and half hours studying daily in the library for a good grade on Comm. 2000 and Dr Wang's history class also, the last two classes I had left to do for the completion of that very sad semester.

I even spent the night in a motel in Turlock studying very hard for the finals and had the written questions down pat. When I received a failing grade after her grade switch I caught on blackboard.

Her evading type e-mails to me, and then I absolutely knew something was obviously wrong and corrupt at CSU STANISLAUS Turlock when I received 50% off right and the wrong answers.

If my final was graded properly I would have passed her class and it would not cost me and our countries taxpayers. This practice costs our state and federal budget thousands of wasted dollars on each student failed on purpose.

That next weeks class Dr Wang wanted me to get the yellow credit non credit slip signed for her to sign. At the same time I grabbed one for Instructor Ashley Albertoni to sign "she declined to sign it". The school then had a physiologist take notes one whole class the week before the May 5th class planned fiasco. I wonder what that shredded report said?

I first made a complaint against Dr. Wang's grade switch to Lee Bettencourt and Denis Shmuck V.P. of faculty when I discovered her grade switch. I did not receive final grade yet at that point.

Denis and lee said I needed to appeal grade and needed to follow the CSU grade appeal rules. The rules say you need to e-mail teacher and give your reason for appeal. "Even though I already had done that to no avail"

I still believe it was my speeches that were all of a political nature was to blame? It was obvious that I was not a bully tea party lover. This is a copy of one of the speeches I wrote and read too the class before the incident I feel she incited on purpose because my vocal non Tea Party political views.

This is an actual speech for Communications 2000 class

Roger De Almeida

Comm. 2000

Prof. Albertoni

Tu & Th 5 to 6:15pm

3/29/2011

Persuasive Outline

"Should the media be censored?"

The evidence is clear, the current news as it is given to the citizens of United States of America and other countries, is biased and a lot of times, just not true. Some news stations and networks have there own agenda and tilts and sometimes misinterpret stories and fabricating some. For example the owners of Fox news and its affiliates are owned by Rupert Murdock and a Saudi Prince Alawleed Bin Talal who blames 911 on the Americans, and a few other radical Republican owners.

When any type of ownership of National media is given to individuals and corporations they are given the power to manipulate and twist the news to there own agenda. One agenda is they want to make President Obama a one time President.
These are some of the lies they are spewing to the vast American public.

The # 1 bullet point is!!! The President was not born in U.S.A., # 2 is that he is a Muslim. This is a national security threat. What they and Rush, Hannity, Palin and other Tea Baggers want you to believe as the truth.

This is bias reporting at best and should not be tolerated or allowed in a country that is at its pivotal crossroads, in our own countries economic turnaround. Facts like weapons of mass destruction ECT... To get us to go to war! It doesn't appear that the misconceptions for the Iraq war would not have happened due to bias reporting. The support to go to war would have been SUBSTANTUALY LOWER if vast U.S. news media viewers weren't bombarded with LIES and misconceptions. Almost ten years gone by, for what?

The people of Iraq and Pakistan are SO poor they didn't do anything to us there regimes did!!!! These people are offered from there own governments or Alcada entices martyrdoms and they will take care of the rest other family's for the rest of their lives.

The fact is that in those countries like Egypt, Tunisia, Iraq and Pakistan the average person makes a salary the equivalent to about $39.00 U.S. dollars a MONTH! That is why suicide bombers are not hard to find. We need to start watching the Media that speaks the truth like MSNBC and are still loyal to ALL citizens equally and not just the rich in this country.

The latest issues the G.O.P leaders are orchestrating a clear sign of what there agenda is they announced an" Emergency meeting to DEFUND FOREVER the N.P.R. national public radio the place where the truth, and what's good news reporting for the average person that's an emergency? What about a jobs making meeting? Or a lets defund the wars effort? if the biased media gets its strong hold on brain washing of there viewers we are all going to be living in a REPUBLICAN MADE, big mess that will be the further downfall of this great country we call the United States of America.

Bibliography;

Michelle Bachman **web sites**

Michelle Bachman speech on March 14 th. Blunder

Ed Shultz show MSNBC

Rachel Meadows show MSNBC

Huffing ton Post

I was and am now clear that instructor Albertoni did not like my political views. That in retrospect reflected on her two faced type e-mails to me. The interactions and the outcome of her changing the class final on her class syllabus after I left the class forcibly said it all.

Nancy and other chairs said I had a merit less non narrative complaint to the grade appeal I had sent to them for review. Well the narrative is Albertoni did not sign yellow credit non credit slip when I asked her to do in front of the class.

That one single act would have alleviated the grade appeal first of all. Second the fact that she did not turn our graded work as graded; instead of giving us all graded work at the end of the semester.

Also the teacher completely changed the final for the reason I appealed in the first place. She gave us students that did not have her e-mailing daily no way to improve our grades or our speeches.

This is what Ashley said in her letter to answer my appeal complaint. Her appeal answers said that she gave individual help to students and input our grades in blackboard. Also saying she imputed grades and did not give our graded work back until a couple weeks before the final speech was due.

This reason and she changing the whole class final was not narrative enough for Nancy and her corrupt chairs to see the truth. The fact is she had to change the final, if she did not do that; the whole class would have failed.

Her incompetence as a University teacher was easily noticed by me. I spent thousands for a community College type learning institutions for years. Now I was paying for a University level teaching at a much higher cost.

Well as I wrote to D.R.S. I hit the trifecta of terrible discriminatory teachers. I also said I was the winner of the CSU gimp horse race. I could not believe the luck I was having with the teachers so far and it was a horrible education to boot.

I was investing thousands of dollars for a degree in a University environment. Needless to say they did not correct the problem. I still think doing the right thing would have been the correct thing to do. The problem is that is not what they want for this country or the school.

The next pages are the actual blackboard grades I printed on May 27th. 2011. Also a copy of the actual grade switches to a lower grade on the 28th Of May 2011. It was adjusted by Dr Wang by just below the needed to pass 70%.

Then copies of the actual midterm miss graded at 50% off right or wrong and in the question answer sheet. This is what we pay thousands of dollars on a single class a semester?

We also are being squeezed for more money for less of an education. And over pay the corrupt administrators more money in some cases move than the vice president of this country!

The government throws away mega money on bad protocols for students and parents. Don't for get the taxpayer's. Instead of the CSU fixing the grading problems for me, they decided to start a crusade to get me expelled at all costs even getting the University police on the crusade.

The ONLY reason for all my complaints were to not be encumbered by overwhelming debt for there mistakes. I did really just not want more unnecessary costs on my student loans. I felt exactly like the younger student protesters at U.C. Davis near my home and wanted nothing less then they were asking for that sad day for democracy for this "The land of the free."

Proof of grade switch and other documents are posted on the book website@ WWW.TeaParty-University.com

CHAPTER 9

Budget busting practices

Well at that point all I had to do is study for Dr Wang's final that was completely miss graded not to mention the previously caught grade switch that also was completely ignored by the CSU. All I wanted was a higher educational experience and fairness for the costly tuition at that CSU. I first sent proof of grade switch D.R.S. office. They said you must take it up with Dr Wang? Dennis said that also. So I e-mailed her and she ignored me again. This was done purposely just to upset me purposely to further there agenda, that I now know for sure now.

So I said I was going to sue the hell out of her and the school. I thought I could help her make the right decision after all I was nice to her even when I first found out she had switched my grades.

By now she went to windy smith for a corrupt and Tea Party Type stance to get me expelled and it worked. No thanks to the Tea Party Proto call of fabricating and taking facts out of context to suit their proof shredding and corrupt ways. She wanted to gamble as did Mr. Hee.

On May 23rd I rented a motel for the final the next day. I was supposed to take the test at the D.R.S. office but decided to take it in class instead and emailed Dr Wang to this. I showed up and she asked me what I was doing there and said I was taking my test as I emailed she left the class and went to her office. She came back after her assistants handed out the final. I was the very first person to finish the final and felt confident I passed. I did pass the class if the final was intently not graded properly as it was. This widely used teacher proto call is what adds to the waste and budget busting school policies. Not to mention the students bottom line budget for higher education degree studies.

I should have known not to challenge the rigged CSU game but I incurred $25, ooo additional fees added to what I owed for absolutely an over paid under higher education costs for nothing and got expelled for using my 1st amendment rights. The only thing I did differently then the student's gas blasted by U.C. Davis is that I complained about the costs and unfair grading policies alone. Windy Smith decided on her own she was going to get me arrested for what she fabricated as did the chancellor of U.C.Davis. The faculty that CSU system has Billions of dollars and the U.C. system has many more billions. This is not enough they must ask for more tuition increases to fund the over paid and under worked, morally challenged faculty and staffs at all California state U.C. and CSU Universities. They are large corporations worth billions and drunk with governmental power!   That needs to change immediately.

I realized I was over my head when the police knocked on my door a minute after Windy hung up on me for the last time. I felt at this point if I was going to be expelled it should be for a valid reason and so I called and said just that and added a few choice words for her. I could imagine the lies she gave to the police on her 911 call that day to have many of them "according to my neighbors" outside within three minutes. She continues to lie as the Tea Party CSU protocol. The Tea Party movement wants to shrink government. Start with taking police power away from ALL schools they are wasting billions. Not to mention miss using the power as in my case and the U.C. Davis gassed students, Penn State and many other abuse of power antic's currently used. If they need police call 911 like we the people do. Campus police should be run as a security company first off! That government cut along with the separate school district cuts on the administrations not the teachers. Administrations that get more money per year per person paid more than the vice president of the U.S. "Over $250.000!"

I went to Senator Steinberg's office after that CSU incited mandatory fiasco, with hope they can fix the problem. I even got her name wrong due to the added stress CSU Stanislaus has crusaded against my 1st amendment rights to me. CSU Windy smith gave her many lies and stonewalled her as she did to me.
The letter bellow is what I wrote to Karen because I got her name wrong;

The Tea Party is ideologists and people in the education sector as all others should not be involved in direct ideology pushing on campus; as abortion and dead babies on strollers as CSU Stanislaus had on campus grounds directly stationed in between classes one afternoon. Fetuses are baby's one sign said! The other sign was of dead bloody babies. Thank god for our U.S. women and there win in Mississippi to have the rights over there own bodies. Here the G.O.P. wants to take food stamps and social security unemployment benefits, welfare and trash them.

Then on the other hand they want any baby even if it stemmed from a rape to be born? Does that make any since at all when the current G.O.P.? The Tea Party wants to shrink government but don't have a democratic plan for our growing population. As a matter of fact they can't even come up with a great plan the 8 years bush and dick were in office. We need up where we are today. The biggest greatest loves hate relationship with this country every body wanted to come here but people are leaving in big numbers. It is not a mass exodus yet because people are stuck in there upside down homes or just plain scared of the future here for them and there family's.

I saw girls crying in the hallways and can here the girls talking about the scare tactics on the campus personal view ideologists. I was so upset over what I was seeing when I was on the way to the library I was stopped by a man with a dead fetus on a stick sign. Before he could utter a word I asked him how many dead babies did he have on his sheets by masturbating over the years.

He simply did not say anything and about ten minutes later they were all gone. I also can't believe they would have a ten foot tall by 7 foot wide photo of Rachel Maddow hung in the library of that right wing run school it was there to fool me and others at that duck crap riddled school. You literally had to watch were you go every step and every day you were there for classes. That should have been a sign looking back.

Governor Brown who was attorney general at the time of the $100.000 paid to Palin for the twenty minute speech. The funds had to be tax dollars despite the Heritage foundations gift to CSU Stanislaus. If it was a gift why did they spend it on a political speech? Why else shred the contract and anything else associated with her payment and the Tea Party.

I even e-mailed the MSNBC Ed Show;

Big Ed,

   Why are we at war and killing for democracy when the world is watching this political theatre? I LOVE THIS COUNTRY! Ed I am having a problem with my University CSU/STAN.EDU the school that paid Palin $100,000 for 20 min speech. I am being expelled 8/12/2011 because I am a liberal and stood up to my 1st amendment rights. I have proof and can fax you. I think this would make for a great segment. The teacher in question is S Wang she first switched my grade and gave me 50% off on my final. This action cost me and the government thousands of dollars in our budget. So I appealed and she shredded the proof and started a witch hunt and it worked because of the TEA BAG show that runs the school. I had Karen from Senator Steinberg's office try to reason with them but they just Ignored her as I. They even called the police on me for standing up for my rights! Something Dr Wang could not have done in her country! Nor could I go to China her Country and be a professor after a year or so. All I want is the same fairness as she received at Michigan State!

Sincerely,

Roger George de Almeida

P.S. This is her website I hope you can help with some answers.

Thanks again and a great job in Wisconsin!

DR Shou Wang

Associate Professor of History

Thanks again and you are doing a great job in Wisconsin for our countries democracy sake!

Dr Wang's Education:

Ph.D., Asian History, Michigan State University, 2002.
Dissertation: Manchu Women in Transition: Gender, Ethnicity, and Acculturation in 17th and 18th Centuries China.
Minor fields: American history; International relations.

M.A., Chinese History, Beijing University, Beijing, China, 1985

B.A., History, Beijing Teacher's College, Beijing, China, 1982

Fields of Interest:

Chinese cultural and social history; Qing history; Gender and ethnicity

Courses Offered:

Course   **Course Title**

HIST 1010   World Civilizations I

HIST 3090   Contemporary World (team-taught)

HIST 3400   Great Teaching (team-taught)

HIST 3800   East Asia in Traditional Times

HIST 3810   East Asia in the Modern World

HIST 4800   Modern China

HIST 4820   Imperial China

HIST 4840   Modern Japan

CHAPTER 10

Fighting for justice

I called Ron Noble only person I could call at CSU according to the expulsion letter and asked for the official answer to the grade appeal for Dr Wang. The next day I had two Sacramento district attorneys come to my door to arrest me for something CSU trumped up? I know this because my neighbors told me they were talking about CSU said that I threatened a teacher! Unless it was to change my grades back it is an outright Lie!

Now I am facing more litigation for standing up to the powerful Tea Party bullies. I hope that I can get a fair outcome but I am afraid of the power they have. I believe in God and believe he will shine and we all will be saved from the doomsday Tea Party approach to governing or lack thereof. They had the GOP DA here in hours after my call not minutes as the last time I know this is a CSU deal because my CSU email was used by DA!

I hope they don't try to give me more problems as I am still trying to get my spinal surgery referral o.k. Thank God also on 11-11-11 I was referred to a surgeon for spine surgery. On 11-22-2011 I received the new surgeon referral I had to fight hard for the corrective surgery.

It was hard to here Michelle Bachman's Titanium rod back speech. Especially when I might be getting that titanium back surgery myself. The problem with the Tea Party and the speeches they give. They are fabricated for the most part. What really gets me upset is when they twist the true American history with their made up history.

Wow who do they think they are?   They are the Tea Party Express from Sacramento, California. I am fighting for fairness something that I never really got from this country's education system from kindergarten to the CSU. My non American physical features and name is foreign too. All this is taking place as the 99% movement started. I am hoping the letter to now Governor Brown below helps my situation in a good way.

11-11-11

Dear, Governor Jerry Brown's office   Attn. Adrian,

I went to schools like Miami Dade College in Florida, Erie College in New York and College of the Desert in Palm desert California and received a Mary Bono Scholarship, San Bernardino College and others over the years. If what CSU Stanislaus-Dr Wang, Windy Smith & Susanne Espinosa crusade was actually true I would have been expelled years ago? They also ignored my complaints that I sent with proof of what Dr Wang did with my class grade to fail me purposely. I was completely ignored on all complaints.

They did not like the fact that I caught them in flagrant federal budget busting scams! The CSU inciting attitude and ignoring the facts and the fabrication of out of context emails to put obstruction of my grade appeal of switched and miss graded budget busting protocols by all CSU's. I fought for my grades to be changed back to the passing grade that was switched. They had this evidence shredded before pushing expulsion thru the other staff. This was the reason for my CSU nightmare they shredded evidence as they did with the yahoo search of the CSU Stanislaus and Sarah Palin after it was too late for me and my CSU experience! Hence this proof sent to Governor Brown.
Also have some ideas of a complete overhaul of the California K-12 curriculum that is partly the Waldorf based teaching method and auditory style along with combinations of Interpersonal style, Kinesthetic-movement methods, and an analytical educational teaching method.

The new public education curriculum I want to put together a complete education overhaul and properly enforced will do away with the current very high drop rate. This negatively affects our state deficit in many different ways. If you are interested I will give you a detailed map to successfully over haul this mess. No child left behind dose exactly the opposite. Teaching for tests and to pass tests no wonder the kids are dropping out at record numbers not to mention that some teachers shouldn't be teachers.

I lived in California since 1968 and California was the worlds 8th largest economy before the Tea Party express came to town! Complete educational changes can be done with the implementation of some key federal legislation. We need to do some VERY drastic changes and it's not Austerity! Its investment in OUR nation building and key other changes. It will be the start of the end of democracy itself if the GOP gets it way! Instead of giving the "so called job creators" free money transfer from Europe and Asia. We still have the largest GDP in the world "let's just use that to our benefit and advantage for once." Instead we are selling our parking meters privatizing toll roads in Colorado and other states are selling OUR infrastructure off while filling just a few individual bank accounts.

These actions are turning back democracy itself and making our county in a bend over state ready to be reamed by China the new communist government super power and we are to blame. They are amassing a bigger war machine then we have the last 10 years. When they nuke us when were off policing the world pushing democracy down other peoples naivety when it is clearly not working now.

The Muslims in Michigan don't even care about voting! The fast media machine these days' shows that Benton Harbor and other are under Communistic type U.S. rule and are being implemented TODAY! You can't vote there you have NO say in your own small town is this the democracy my friends and other Americans died for?

The world in minutes sees what our Tea Party express and the corrupt banking system are doing to the world's economy not just ours. If the Tea Party gets the majority and wins the white house I feel as many economists and business billionaires like Miss Tilton who owns a couple big businesses here in California and others say there is going to be another revolution if nothing is done soon. It has now started in the birth place of Democracy Itself "Greece". For now our democracy is still the best in the world; but not for long if the current government doesn't change "I don't mean Obama". We are showing the greed of the one percent to the world right now! We need to spend our way out of this "and not with on the war machine"

CSU higher education is an expensive investment and endeavor and should have lasting good memories of what you paid all that money for. The merit less education the CSU Stanislaus provides for the unlucky students of the obviously corruptly ran school. I am sure any student would be upset if you were expelled statewide for appealing grades that were undeniably changed and miss graded. For standing up to that real Tea Party run school the real school of BULLIES movement!

I got expelled and they tried to get me arrested on August 10th 2011 for using and standing up to my 1st amendment rights! School was out May 24th and DRS and V.P Denis excused me from that as email states. They kept what was supposed to be a short appeal process into months of stress added to what they knew of my medical condition. They purposely added stress even after I reminded them various times. Some thing in there own appeal rules say they flagrantly did not follow themselves.

They also knew I was in a lot of pain and need spinal surgery from the note from my surgeon. They absolutely by the calls and emails all those months was to make me and managed to stress me out pretty bad and make my health worse. They finally broke me at that point and I did not care if that corruptly ran school expelled me. The problem is it was CSU system wide not just the most corrupt CSU Stanislaus. I get this unjust outcome reversed to what should have been done.

I have actually surpassed the 70% passing grade for my fulfillment of the course objectives on Dr Wang's syllabus. If Dr Wang did not miss grade and change grades for my failure and added thousands to my student loans and federal budget. I would have not been upset or as bad off as I am today. If they did this to me they have done this to many other younger students. If I new they were a tea Party school I would have NEVER matriculated there. I did because of there Portuguese culture studies and I am Portuguese and thought it would be better than Sac States protocols.

How could I have been disruptive and harassing threatening at school when all I Wanted and the Header of the e-mails sent that they twisted and out of context wand. Some proof was shredded before going on to the different departments except for Brett Conner history chair over Dr Wang. After I sent proof of her discriminated grading polices do and did to me. All I wanted was FAIRNESS; the semester was already over.

Even Eric Forbes from CSU chancellor's office long beach Ca. said "I was not even on campus or used there campus computer as in the letter of statewide expulsion?"

They also out right lied to Dept of Education Rick Allen he has been trying to help me get fairness also. Not to forget stonewalling Karen at Senator Steinberg's office. I just want fairness and my grades put back to what I worked for; a passing 70% grade. They also sent me and the whole school that Ricky Martin died that made the CSU experience worse for me not to mention how I felt.

I know him personally, and I worked with him. I enclosed just a few commercials I did. I also met President Clinton and I worked for Senator Paul Gordon and his writer wife. And I lived with a FBI agent in Malibu and my nephew's father is L.A.P.D. veteran that died of cancer not to long ago. My grandfather was a Constable on Patrol also for decades.

Adrian I dwindled down proof for you if you need more let me know. Please excuse my own doctor scribbled notes for myself. I hope you can at least get my correct grades for that semester and get Sac State to actually drop as per my drop slip for the whole last semester do to injuries sustained in the car accident July 2009. I do not want litigation for I am still in enough. If you get to see the entire original dated schools emails to me you will know the real truth. I also have other civil maters that were derived by my bad injury that I am also currently trying to rectify also.

Thanks again,

Roger George de Almeida

A very important key to my being expelled was that Lee Bettencourt gave my private medical records and broke doctor patient confidentiality laws. And gave to Dennis, Susanne and windy to use against me for there corrupt agenda.

All the problems of the current economy left me homeless in 2008 as I stated before. Well since Sac state labeled me as bipolar witch is not true. They took what I know to be a mid life crises and it was compounded by all the accident and hardships of the past few very hard years have done to me.

Also because of the spinal Injury sustained in the car accident I was not in school and not receiving scholarships and loans I needed to survive. I would have not been receiving if it were not for me being badly injured.

I also was afraid of losing another house. I just purchased my house and I felt I needed to get some business cards and was planning on paying up my back contactors license fees after doing a couple handyman jobs from what I thought were friends.

I was summons to go to small claims court and they won a judgment and two liens were placed on my house for non completion of jobs. The reason for not completing the 6 hours work needed to finish was simple.

Jon the owner of condo was on a two week cruise and was e-mailing Todd "the project manager" daily job changes. The job changes were many and told them that it would cause more budget problems for the money left for me for materials.

It was close to finishing when I told him that I needed to use all the money given to me to finish and the rest of Dave's marble money also! Before Jon got back "they said do whatever you need to do so you can get over Dave's." They certainly had to have this planned!

I installed Granite slab counter tops in kitchen, exotic bamboo wood floors in hallway and kitchen they added a custom shower instead of the tub as agreed before he left; that added a lot more work and materials to the original amount. I kept all receipts and went over about $1,500. Dave gave me $1,300 Dave and I never got paid!

I kept the grouting and pluming to be done until I got paid. That way I could give Jose the worker doing all heavy work due to my injury. The day came when Jon returned home from his two week cruise and Todd was supposed to pick him up at San Jose airport. "That is a few minutes away from his apartment"

Todd and Jon decided to not square away the issues and go over the receipts to that point. Instead they both went to Todd apartment in San Francisco deliberately. So I could not go over receipts and finish the few hours left for completion. Not only did Todd kick and break material he threatened that I must finish Jon's job even though I was not going to be paid for all the materials or work done!

While being verbally abusive and breaking things, Todd also threatened I was going to be taken to court by Dave! I not only lost in small claims court they put a lien on my house to for $2,200. So not only did I increase the value of his condo by at least $23.000. The judge said I did all that work for free and I was to pay him$2,200 in form of a lien on my house.

I was also sued by Jose the helper that also did not get paid. I was sued buy his friend Dave also, who's money was put into Jon's condo with his permission while his friend was on a two week cruise.

For all that work Jose and I did was done for free by law apparently and to pay him back for adding thousands of dollars to his condo? This new court proceeding must be a CSU retribution for going to the governors office and blowing the whistle on their budget busting and corrupt ways. For the same thing happened to me in Fresno small claims court and Mark Sharp got no arrest warrant! Just I did?

So now I am being charged for working without the license I paid into for years. This was only a jog for a friend the cost and circumstances prove that. And that's why the CSU sent the DA to my house that morning of the governors meeting.

I am now facing jail time even though Jon and Todd kept me from paying Dave for his material money back. The judge also put two liens against my house, one for Jon for $2,200 and one for $1,300 for Dave. I do believe that should be UN lawful in itself.

It is just as the Lacey's did to me years before that how I know it was a set up! They all have degrees and must have had it planned for the free work performed. We also had no signed contract because it was job for a friend! Something I would have never done if it were a regular job "besides the friend price."

I was a licensed contactor for over 15 years until I lost it all due to the bad economy. Never once did I have a complaint until Dave, Todd and Jon's fabrications and perjury in court. I only can hope to straighten this out in court again."

I hope to get justice this time around"

So far I have close to $58,000 in student loans with a payment of over $500.00 a month. It is too much of a loan balance to be just half way to a Bachelor's degree. Our country's huge educational costs are a burden to most.

The last Brazilian President had only a 4th grade education and grew up poor. He understood what the disparity in income was doing to his country. He was governing his country for what was needed to be remedied to have the economy grow and expand for the growing population. "Sound familiar?"

These problems are just a couple reasons why Brazil and China are striving competition for world leader in GDP and economics. Not to mention our polarities are bought in our political auctions for quid pro quo.

Well what the Brazilian President ended up doing was give every family 150$00 Brazilian Reals to each child aprox $100.00 U.S. dollars a month.

After only a few months people started buying things they could not afford before. Items like General Electric home appliances, cars ECT...and it's been booming ever since. There is also a smart Brazilian that got into the business of offshore oil and is producing oil for about twenty U.S. dollars a barrel. We also can do that too if we put our minds to it!

They can do the same here but corporations know the U.S. citizens will accept anything they come up with and say. This is not a democracy or what our forefathers had in mind or wanted for this country. If they can see what is happening to this country they would certainly have a cow!

America with a plan will be right on top again; the GOP and status quo will run us certainly to the ground in time. The GOP has had there chance and all they did is get us in a made up war that made dick Chaney a billionaire!

Dick Chaney became very wealthy with the taxpayers money from the inside deals made for Halliburton and the made up war. Dick and Bush also get away with gross war crimes and made everybody hate Americans again. The elitist views of the GOP ideology will end democracy itself.

The GOP has tried for many years now, their devised Trickle down system for money extraction. It only works for the 1 percent. It is not working and has not worked for our economy since Bush 41 was in office. It is just a one trick pony on the society. All just to make the middle class go down on the American Dream ladder.

The truth is we need to do a massive two trillion dollar stimulus plan but with a tax overhaul and reinstate the banking regulations deregulated by GOP and the Bushes. Make all the too big to fail banks sell off and making them the size they were back in the 70's.

Take ALL the money out of politics as Dylan Ratigan and the 99% protest against. That way politicians only get a salary no more private donations No inside trading actions or buy outs or quid Pro Quo trades, changing laws for easy money extracting.

Chapter 11

Making the Government Smaller

The fact is since Bush administration the government doubled in size. Achieving there ideology by taking this country hostage politically. Also simultaneously trying to set us back over fifty years along with the middle class, by annulling laws that worked in the past.

Overboard GOP bullying forced the big protests like the Tea Party and now 99% protests. The other poverty stricken and middle class people's campaign for the civil inequality and the journey for a better America.

One million African humans were scattered across the Atlantic Ocean that got sick and were thrown overboard on the slave ships. They were on the way for the progress of this country we now call the United States of America. The GOP Tea party is changing the course of this great country's history.

Meanwhile in China the process of trying to over take our superpower status is spreading like a wild fire. While we are policing the world on our dime and they are doing this with the money we borrowed from them that they made from U.S. in the first place.

China is building a naval fleet larger than the United States currently has at this time in history. They also have a massive amount of air power and just bought an aircraft carrier from Russia to boot.

Instead of getting our government in order Kevin McCarthy and Tea Party Express in "you tube" the Tea Party garbage yourself. This new tea party ideology is the beginning to the end of democracy itself.

The tea party and McCarthy truly believes in the need of ending the 1933 law for Wall Street. This to further the self regulating laws that keep the money from being invested improperly in the first place. If they get there way not even a delicatessen will be able to stay open for business as usual.

The GOP government is making the big mistake it made in the past; witch is the mixing crony capitalism with Democracy. They say that 47% have no work that the real learning continues at home. This statistic also must change in the educational process and in the economic inequality problem we face again as a country.

The G.O.P. government is putting the label of socialist on the president. The bullying is in the lucky sperm club and is part of the 1%. Norquist went to the Nixon school of politics and trickery. The Los Angeles power hungry crew he fed quid pro quo!

Norquist seems to have all that power with a signature contract. Supposedly there is no expiration date for that political mistake. How things have changed and the country is held hostage by a new tricky Dick Norquist. "Since when do the lawmakers abide to any contract including the one they make with their constituents?"

Every place we put ground troops for war purposes in our history we are still there today! For example we are in Germany, Korea, Vietnam everywhere we went to war we are still there. We cannot continue this stance or we will lose the time and resources to get our house in order. It is not too late to solve the problems the United States faces in our economy and our banking problems.

The G.O.P. 2006 lame duck Congress again legislated there own self Interest made up laws. They passed laws for the U.S. Postal service to pay into different bank accts for a seventy year fund for retirement. Now what other private or government run business does that? "None" That is the only thing that is wrong with the post office.

And social security problem is that congress took money from both interests to fund the out of control war costs. We seem to have no control on the cost and never had or have a real strategy to get out. By destroying them they don't have to put the money back they used on the needless war.

I personally would like to know "are the banks paying the property taxes on those houses staying unoccupied due to the fraudulent loans they made in recent past. Also car insurance companies let the taxpayers pay for most all car accident emergency hospital and Ambulance costs.

Not to forget the very expensive unnecessary Surgeries? This dishonest practice cost our government and us taxpayers lots of needless waste also. That's what our government should do away with. "Not the democratic social fallback intuitions we all pay into and fought for."

The Tea Party is pro life so how are we going to have the recourses for the new population when they want to get rid of government as we know it. Their ideology will wipe out the many years of history and the fight for a true democracy.

One thing we can do for starters to save all our public schools and the high cost universities. We first need to make sure teachers are there to help educate not to pay off there student loan by teaching.

We need to give a surprise profiling questionnaire to test to all teachers, faculty and staff of any universities. This will have a lasting great impact on the education that we are all over paying for now.

Then due to the Tea Party University discriminatory practices on myself, and many others that just were silenced or fell through the cracks. Windy smith decided to criminally incite with the discriminatory practice of editing out of context the emails ECT...

That Wendy should be charged with trying to get someone falsely arrested. Windy is a felon in training not to mention obstruction of justice; the job she is paid by the taxpayer to do.

Knowing that a conviction can keep you from obtaining a good job needed from achieving any higher educational career goals. This is simply too much power for any one person to have especially to a knowingly corrupt school administration as the CSU Stanislaus campus and others.

My third grade teacher was so whacked out she makes Professor Shou Wang from CSU Stanislaus look like a saint. Not to mention the recorded call to 911 operators falsely made by Windy Smith to falsely have me arrested at my own home? Also why did the school decide to go the distance to try to stop my further education?

The Tea Party's slowly taking democracy itself away from "We the People." "The patriot acts" that new law is used by government entities to trample on people they see fit "even law abiding citizens of our own country without due coarse. That's why Obama was elected! Change we wanted but did not get!

My rights and the rights of students and future students is what I am fighting so hard for. We were completely and purposely ignored by the corrupt administrations. Or by who sabotaged the truth of the CSU operated university police.

The paying students of UC Davis and I have a constitutional and fundamental democratic right to have peaceful demonstrations for justice. Their own grade appeal laws and regulations ask for you to explain you grievance with the teacher who purposely failed you in the first place.

I called and talked with Dennis VP of faculty and he said I needed to email Dr. Wang again and explain why she should change my grades back from what they were!! Windy smith's explanation is obscured and a fabrication of what actually happened.

Shue Wang's use of discriminatory grading policy's at best; just marking half off "true or not true" is issuing an automatic failing grade! Something I feel she has done over and over from some of the other classmates harsh comments.

Or in my case wanting honest education and grades that I paid top dollar for. These type practices are a big burden on me and the government." Doing this practice "just on a hundred or so students" and you have enough to pay $100,000 to Palin for a dumpster diver speech!

The money supposedly was donated specifically to pay for a speech from Palin, to a University? Why and how is this legal? Google it like I did it made me sick! For what they spent thousands for when our state and federal budgets are out of control! And they want austerity?

I wonder what happened to the CSU dumpster divers who made it in the 100 k speech. What was put together and given with help paid for and by taxpayers? There is no logical reason to the ideological changes we are being subject to nowadays. The world population is at an all time high and we are going to cut back? This is Economics 101 danger!

Chapter 12

Politics and Universities

The night of the well paid Palin visit there was about one hundred protesters outside the CSU School. Raising up a Sarah Palin shaped piñata saying "spill baby spill" and "Open the Books." she said "She was expecting the protests" and some of her supporters were there too. There were about thirty people carrying signs that read "support free speech."

I have been getting those old nightmares on fairness and hopelessness again. The bad dreams I started having about Dr Wang, and the politically run administration and the type of or lack thereof of educating students. These quagmires inspired me to write this book.

It is clear to me that CSU STANISLAUS is using the same cruel tea party tactics. They also were making up out of context emails from me to create the situation to expel me. "It Worked"

If there are any fellow classmates of Seventh Street School in San Pedro, California in early 1970's that remember the temple squeezer or John. Also if any class mates of comm. 2000 Albertoini or Dr Wang' history 1000 class at CSU Stanislaus or any other situation from abuse from a teacher or staff of any school please send a letter to your local representatives.

Recently I watched a local news segment of a Sacramento school administration used a surveillance camera to expel a well known male cheerleader for kissing another male. A lot of people got outraged and the school reinstated him.

Teachers and administrations know the rules and know how they could get away with changing them. Dr Wang and the temple squeezer got away with should be criminal. It was also clear to me that our class was not the only one to get Dr. Wang's Chinese method of 50% off right or wrong answers for her grading method just as they cheat on her Expatriate currency.

We are in a world where our current population is seven billion. Today's long lasting wars has had a huge negative impact on our economy. Not to mention the world economy which the American dollar is used to purchase world market commodities and other wall street junk and very risky paper sold.

Paul Ryan is known to be negatively spinning Obamas fight for the middle class. He fabricates and jokes about how its Obamas war against the middle class. The fact is the heritage foundation and Bush and Dick that started both wars even the one on the middle class.

It's the tea party ideology that started the middle class warfare years ago. Now the Tea Party is pushing forward with worse inequality issues and laws. Ryan furthermore states in his speech's that it makes this country weaker not stronger! Get a clue Ryan Plan!

So what that says is, that they know exactly what the tea party is causing to the world economy and don't care! Dirty water dirty air, more war and hunger and needless disparity and totally out of control crime to boot. Is that what we want for this country's near future?

The chamber of commerce has been a good part of government until they conspired with the Tea Party ideology. They completely were bought and as corrupt as the current auction government. Our factories need to be retooled for manufacturing our technical products we invent here in United States.

Even Steve jobs would agree that he tried hard but could not find factories in the U.S. to make his Ipad. He had to go to china to make his ipad. Add one more of the many intellectual properties knocked off.

Jobs and other American Corporations are going overseas and china instead of here. Paul Ryan also says Obamas is going to town to town creating divisive redirect.

Paul Ryan and other GOP also said Obama used broken politics of the past straw-men and escape- goats and engaging in intellectually lazy arguments. "He has mesmerizing eyes but looking into them don't make you stupid"

Most all the pro American and Americas heritage foundation, Alec, Tea Party Express, Americans for ECT... What these groups are actually doing is the opposite what people think they are doing usually.

Like the pro choice movement for example "Mostly based on lies and bully tactics." We are close to a 7 billion population and if we continue governing this way we are going loose our current top superpower status. Our U.S. credit rating was downgraded because these Tea Party Bullies did not care at all of the consequences.

These are the same bully and scare tactics they are using for the end of women rights. All the things some women fought and died for years ago to have. Just one more war the GOP initiated recently.

The "bonus army" protests of the Hoover administration are similar of what's taking place all over again today for the 99% protesters. All we want is fairness in life in this democracy.

What we need as a democratic country is jobs for the masses and for the current population growth. It is necessary NOW to spend "trillions" on getting the new econometric rolling. Just about the same spent on the made up War of Iraq.

A massive investment needs to be spent in our own nation building. We have desperately needed to start infrastructure expansion and rebuilding. We also need newly created incentives for retooling our factories for our own technology.

These new and old factories retooled and orientated in manufacturing the intellectual products and patents invented here and to be made in the U.S.A. again. We then can start re purchasing our 50,000 closed U.S. factories that closed in the eight Bush and Dick Chaney regime trickle down years.

If we could only come together as the U.S. superpower that we are, we will do well as we done before... The U.S. should spend the same or more than we needlessly wasted on Iraq war "approximately 2.4 Trillion dollars." We can immerge from this other man made economic nightmare.

If this nation building expenditure of our own is not going to happen soon it will be the ruin of all that we as a free nation worked over 200 years for. This would also hit the world economy in the ripple effect that has already started to do.

The current elitist ideology of a few ultra rich morally challenged people also known as the 1%. They are taking this country to its knees and its democracy hostage. Preferential treatment was the C- University student called President Bush # 43.

Part of keeping World superpower status and true democracy is to get our 50.000 factories back open again. We can accomplish this with a renewed crusade for the "Made in America stamp."

"We the People" don't mind paying more for that stamp. Like big Ed says all we need to do is give them the same tax incentives lobbied to come back as the bush administration gave them to leave this country.

The key element of our country doctrine is the U.S. Constitution. All the different amendments that accompany it are being dissected by the tea party GOP.

Can the Tea Party really put them selves in another human's mind or shoes? They also lack the morals and empathy needs to make the right choices to govern for our fast growing nation.

They also seem to be blind to the human rights laws altogether. Is it that the tea party just has blinders on or is this just a part of a much bigger master plan to turn this country in time and history?

Virginia Fox is right; there is no reason for students to be $100,000 in debt. The cost of an education rose 900% since she was able to work her way up the ladder of success. The diploma she holds was also much easier to obtain in the 1960's. American students are currently about 1 trillion dollars in debt. This is out of control when the actual cost of education is very low due to the worlds current computer age.

The GOP is using our nine Trillion deficits that the GOP governing got us too in the first place, as the reason for austerity. This is now holding back our countries capabilities of coming out of this in a few years instead of twenty or thirty.

Bush and the GOP did to our first time deficit surplus that Clinton made for this country. They don't really care about regular Joe citizens. Starting or spending trillions of dollars on a made up war.

When and if they really do care about this great country and world we all share, we will see and feel the differences. It is essential to strengthen the future of the working middle class and keeping the superpower status we have today.

Instead we are losing 1% to 2% GDP per year or more needlessly. People need to wish for our nation building to happen soon. This for the so? of the wonderful democratic government we all already fought died and is continuing dieing for today!

What teachers are doing now is teaching "cheating." Cheating is in the teaching in our schools for years since no child left behind. If your schools test percentages are down so is the funding of your school. So they willingly cheat to achieve bigger budgets for their school district. Many teachers have publicly admitted to this practice.

So teachers do some manipulation of grades as Dr Wang did to me. "If it happened to me than it happened to many other students." After all Teachers is an anagram of "Cheater."

The cheating in the money in education seems to be luring the wrong type of teachers. This is the wrong picture to be teaching to our countries future. Trust the teacher as you would the feeling of greed.

We all seem to learn the hard way sometimes. As Brad Pitt said recently Socialism is not a bad word or bad government. Actually it is narrowly what true Democracy should have parts of. My sentiment of this government stands exactly the same as current mayor of Lansing, Michigan Virg Burnero of Boston, Mass.

The very courts that are giving corrupt verdicts are ramped up lately. For example; Maytag Company was sold to whirlpool and then they stopped paying them and they went to court in 2011and lost.

Now the same government wants the us postal service to come up with seventy years worth of retirement benefits. Just so they can extract the money out and piece it away as Romey did in his last job. That job taking apart businesses made him a multi millionaire.

This type economics and hundreds of thousands unemployed is what got us to this point. This is how the Tea Party government wants to help get us out of this economy? They want to make us all sitting ducks in wetlands with oil slicks in the United States of America the "mad max type of living."

The 1995 inception of META "banks regulating themselves" this new law stopped completely the way we kept our property records since the beginning of America. Also this created the huge deficits in all U.S. counties. This by taking the fees out of recording county to county and state to state.

These laws were changed by banks and Wall Street to be able to gamble with our nation's future. The havoc that we see today from the predatory man made banking laws. "This by praying on mostly the uneducated and poor." This is immorality and a complete crime to our nation's democracy.

Of purposely giving away bad loans that resulted in costly foreclosures to the economy. No new bank loans to repurchase even though our tax dollars bailed them out. Also the millions of jobs lost in the real estate and construction industry. This made people go back down the ladder of success like myself.

The Transitional Kindergarten was added to the California curriculum in the November 2011 California elections. The new law makes the start age cut off in September not December to start kindergarten. If we can implement this new law we can change the whole system as needed now.

Why not implement a law for the Waldorf teaching method for greater positive response to education and making learning fun. That is one change it will take to save our drop out rate causes.

If we can let the teachers teach! Not for passing tests but actually teach our country. This will be better for all the generations to come, our future Governors, Senators, Congress, and presidents to come.

Why not do as Michelle Kwee did in Washington schools. We can get rid of the wasted money on the ineffectual teachers. It was working! But it would have stopped the wasteful stays Quo so the teacher's federation spent a million dollars to get her terminated.

CHAPTER 13

"The U.S. Government hid what?"

In the many days researching for the accuracy of facts in this book, I became aware of what the U.S. government was doing secretly to forgotten children. These atrocities were happening about the same time the elementary school nightmare "corporeal punishment" occurred for me in California.

It is now 2012 and we have 20 states that still use the paddle and let teachers do what they please to our children. For more info and free magazines for teachers go to Tolerance.org

Child predators like some school coaches and the temple squeezers of the educational institutions. They need to be regulated from an outside entity that does surprise visits to all schools public and private.

It will not catch all the bad things going on but will stop some and will defiantly make for the big changes. This is necessary for keeping some child predators away from those important and trust worthy jobs. They put a bad rap on the good teachers. People like that teacher in L.A. had been molesting and getting away with t for years.

The CSU sent more police to my house, this time two investigators from the District attorneys office in Sacramento, California the Tea Party headquarters.

I feel I am over my head with this school and they are using the CSU police "windy Smith" to scare me and it worked. I have to turn myself in San Bruno Jail next week and want to finish editing this book before I go turn myself in.

I asked the San Francisco District attorneys office who put the complaint in? And they said it was the State of California. The CSU Stanislaus sent them here "I am sure of that" It happened the day I called Ron Noble.

The police motto is "to protect and to serve" not for Penn State, U.C. Davis, Sac State or CSU Stanislaus for that matter. The corrupt Penn State CSU administrations are in many different parts of education.

Newt Gingrich might agree publicly to some of the Furnald practices. I on the other hand was dumbfounded and sick to read the following facts. Especially what is going on even now in education? The fact that hit me hard was that the boy who came out publicly is Portuguese and shares my same last name and heritage.

"Eugenics" our government together with the proctor and gamble Corporation. The medieval practice of using some Massachusetts students in a male orphanage called "furnald" as radioactive chemical testing guinea pigs.

The following is from the book is called "The State Boys Rebellion."

"The State Boys Rebellion,"

Fred Boyce was just 8 years old in 1949 when his foster mother died, and the State of Massachusetts committed him to Fernald. Boyce's records from Fernald show they labeled him as a "moron", even though tests showed his intelligence was within the normal range, not bad for a boy with no education at all. He was kept there for 11 years.

Boyce says he thinks the state recommended that he come to Fernald because it was the easy way out: "They didn't have to look for homes for you, so they could just dump you off in these human warehouses and just let you rot, you know. That's what they did. They let us rot."

Most of the school is closed now, including Boyce's old dorms, which will be torn down soon. Approximately 36 children slept in each room, with the beds jammed together.

"The State Boys Rebellion,"

And the children received little education and less affection. Regimentation? There was no shortage of that. And how long would they stay at Fernald?

The kids were told they could be here for life, that there was no exit. "I kind of thought for a while, maybe there was something wrong with me, or why would I be here," says Joe Almeida, who was swept up into the system even though there was nothing wrong with him.

Almeida, an abused child, was only 8 when his father took him for a drive to the Fernald School, and told him to wait in the hallway." I said, 'Wait a minute, dad. Where are you going,'" recalls Almeida. "He goes, 'Oh, you wait right there. I got to go get the car." And he went. And that was the last I seen of him."

"The State Boys Rebellion,"

Almeida had no idea where he was, and no idea that he now wore an invisible label, which read "moron." He ended up in the same dorm as Boyce, and they spent their mornings in the" schoolroom." At least, that's what the room was called.

"It was a school in name only. A child would experience the first year of school 5 or 6 times in a row," says D'Antonio. "He would read the same 'Dick and Jane' reader, and never make any progress because the school wasn't equipped to actually educate children. It was there as a sort of holding pen."

"The State Boys Rebellion,"

D'Antonio, who adds that the school made sure that at least 30 percent of the kids "The State Boys Rebellion," admitted had normal or near normal intelligence. The school needed those kids to work. "You had to have somebody with a certain level of intelligence in order to run this place," says Boyce. "And I can remember being out in the gardens from morning until night in the sun."

The children did most of the manual labor at the school. "The kids at Fernald raised the vegetables that they ate. They sewed the soles on the shoes that they wore.

They manufactured the brooms that they used to sweep the floor," says Almeida, however, had an unusual job, and the fruits of his labor are still there 50 years later.

"The State Boys Rebellion,"

His job was to cut up the brains of severely retarded people who had died at Fernald. He cut them into thin slices so scientists could study them.

Nothing ever came of the research, but the bits of brains are still there. "They're still sitting here years later," says Almeida. "I mean, what was it all for?" Worse than the work, says Almeida, was the abuse he suffered from the attendants who staffed the place.

It was called "Red Cherry Day," and the kids would sit in a circle and be called up alphabetically. "And lucky me, my name is what? Almeida. You'd get up in front of all these kids, and you would pull down your pants," recalls Almeida.

"The State Boys Rebellion,"

"You'd pull down your underpants and they'd make you turn around and they'd whack your ass with this branch until it was red like a cherry." Almeida says few of the attendants showed any kindness, and Some of them should have been institutionalized themselves:

"These people were sick that worked here."

And of course, there was sexual abuse. The place was tailor made for it.

"The State Boys Rebellion,"

As the boys grew older, many rebelled, often by running away. They always got caught. Boyce showed Simon what happened then. The kids were taken to the infamous Ward 22, the school's detention center. "Couldn't escape, you know, this was the prison," says Fred, who was locked up in solitary confinement here. "And they had a little mattress on the floor there."

As a further humiliation, kids were stripped naked. Back then, the windows had bars. "You're just this child, and you're in this cell because you ran away," says Boyce. "And you ran away for reasons of abuse and thinking that you don't belong here. You wanna have a life outside."

"The State Boys Rebellion,"

Boyce finally got that life in 1960, when he was 19. " Eugenics" was no longer politically acceptable in America, and Fernald started releasing people.

The problem was, there weren't a lot of jobs around for alumni of a school for the feeble-minded. Boyce joined the carnival circuit, traveling around the country, mixing with people who didn't need to see diplomas – surrounded by reminders of what his childhood could have been.

"I see these happy families, you know, and I see how much they love their kids. And I think, you know, 'I can never have that,'" says Boyce. What would their lives have been like, if they hadn't been sent to Fernald?

"The State Boys Rebellion,"

"The one thing I can imagine is that their lives would have had a lot more love in them. I've had men tell me, 'I never saw a man or woman who loved each other growing up."

I never saw family life. And it's been impossible for me to find it as an adult,'" says D'Antonio. "That's the part that gets me most upset, is they were denied the human relations that sustain all of us."

Almeida got out of Fernald the same year as Boyce, but when he hit his 40s, he found himself drawn back to the place. It was the only home he'd ever really known. But Fernald had changed, and only the seriously handicapped were living there now. So Almeida applied for a job and worked there as a driver for 20 years. He retired last year.

"The State Boys Rebellion,"

"I always felt like they owed me. I always felt that they owed me, because they took the most important thing of my life away," says Almeida. "They took away my childhood and my education.

The two things that you need in life to make it, they took from me. "And that's not all. More than 30 years after Boyce and Almeida were released, they found out that the school had allowed them to be used as human guinea pigs.

In 1994 Senate hearings, it came out that scientists from MIT had been giving radioactive oatmeal to the boys - men now - in a nutrition study for Quaker Oats. All they knew is that they'd been asked to join a science club. Among those who attended the hearing was Almeida, also a member of the club.

"The State Boys Rebellion,"

He says the boys were recruited with special treats: "We were getting special treatment, you know, extra dessert, we got to eat away from the other boys. We were getting extra oatmeal. We're getting extra milk."

"But they forgot to mention the milk was radioactive," says David White-Lief, an attorney who worked on the state task force investigating the science club.

He says he was outraged that the children were exploited without their knowledge. "It's my contention, and it was my contention on the task force, that these experiments, because of the lack of informed consent, violated the Nuremburg Code established just 10 years earlier," says White-Lief.

"The State Boys Rebellion,"

"The lesson of Nazi Germany was we don't do experiments on people without informed consent. They didn't use the word "informed consent" - without knowing consent." Boyce, also in the science club, got a group of members together and they sued.

Each received approximately $60,000 in compensation from MIT, Quaker Oats and the government. But Boyce and Almeida never got what they really wanted: an apology for sending them to Fernald and calling them morons, a label that remains on their state records to this day.

"The State Boys Rebellion,"

Boyce, who is 63, says he has never received an apology from the State of Massachusetts or from any agency at all. What stays with him the most, says Almeida, is being labeled a moron, and "never getting to know what I could have been." Today kids like Fred Boyce and Joe Almeida are placed in foster homes and attend public schools.

The dark era of institutionalization ended in the '70s at Fernald. Since then, it's become a home for mentally and physically handicapped adults, and it's about to be closed down forever.

The publisher of the book, "The State Boys Rebellion," is Simon and Schuster. Both Simon and Schuster and **CBSNEWS** are units of Viacom.

My nightmares from my K-6 public education and abuse came to the surface recently. Remembering and reliving the swats form that ugly whole ridden paddle. That's another reason I wrote this book "to get the truth of the bad parts much needed to be repaired our U.S. educational system.

To me CSU Stanislaus reopened my own "FERNALD NIGHTMARE." Current teachers are in need of peer evaluations from an outside entity with surprise visits. I personally feel highly of the efficient teachers currently registered in the ninety thousand National Board of teachers.

It just takes Nine hundred a fraction of bad apples to need to spoil the basket! We need to "throw the bad ones away to make sure the rest of the bucket of apples doesn't spoil." This is just part of the overhaul needed for the United States educational system.

Racism and poverty also plays a major roll in the achievement gaps, from kindergarten thru the higher education institutions. Ineffective teachers also are key to an unhealthy class.

If a teacher can't engage kids to use critical thinking tools and don't use the multitude of teaching techniques. The many methods as mentioned previously that we can use to solve the issues needed. The most statistically best teaching technique is the Waldorf method. Also the combinations of all teaching methods together in every school day. This would be an optimal change in education.

Chapter 14

For democracy's sake

The "Project follow thru" was a step in the right direction in 1967. $120 million in 1967 dollars was proposed by President Lynden Johnson's administration. This infusion of money in the public school system to help with disadvantaged children! Congress appropriated $15 million only and the whole project was cut down and did not work even though they only changed the law in 1995.

Also "reading is important." The implementation of certain tools as the federation of teacher's wants us to believe. The implementations they never get around to do on purpose. Making the necessary changes to overhaul our educational system.

For instance putting a million dollars in the election to get rid of Michelle Kwee, the woman that came very close to single handling our entire public educational systems problems. Another GOP democracy changing lip ness test like voter suppression.

It is important to have the parents to teach our kids. It is just some teachers that don't understand some parents are not capable of teaching there kids. Why are some teachers blaming the parents? Parents don't get paid to teach there kids they do what they can for free.

It is part of being a parent, just some parents do not have the means to buy or have the learning tools. The tools necessary for there kids important early mind development.

It is my current fight is advocating eradicating corrupt school administrations. From K-12 to the higher learning educational institutions. Also to reform the entire system just as Michelle Kwee started too.

The surprise in class peer evaluations should help psychologically force the bad teachers to do a much better job. From such evaluations, we will come to understand the teaching weaknesses and strengths that they have and could not see themselves.

"Ineffective teachers must go tenure or not."

We have "toys for tots" and other poverty stricken American charity drives. Why can we not give the teaching tools for families that can't afford the early learning videos and the tools that go with them?

It will save our children future and the future of this country. Just look what happened to our U.S. government and most of its branches. They are mostly corruptly run with self interests that are criminal to most every body else in our democratic social fabric.

For example we pay fulltime salaries for Congressmen, Senators, judges, mayors, governors, and presidents in our government. But they are on the phone more than half the time raising money for the next election. When they should be solving our huge problems we put them in office to solve in the first place.

Some politicians have morals and love this country. For most of the 99% know that the current problems were self made. Caused by nothing more than greed and from quid pro quo deals that extracts our tax money and democracy itself.

"Freedom of speech" should be just that FREE. It should not be sold and just given to the highest bidder. Our countries politicians became politicians for money and power. Not for the best interests of this current superpower and awesome Country millions of Americans rich, middle class and poor call home.

For instance political running mates like Sarah Palin and hey $100.000"Dumpster diving" and "bendable straws" type speeches. To the mega Millions spent on a road to nowhere as to her fake run for president for 2012.

Just running made her a multi millionaire over night not to mention the Tea Party power that went with it. It worked so well for her until old Newt got in it as well. A real democratic Government should run for the people. Not for too big to fail banks and corporations. If mitt Romney is right about corporations being people then why not let them all fail?

Don't get me wrong, I love capitalism, money and the ladder to success. The problem is it needs to be on an even playing field. Something apparently today politicians don't care about at all.

Letting the housing and banking frauds continue on without prosecution. For some are in high positions still are just compounding our now global issues and problems without accountability. Also if Mitt says corporations are American people? Then why are they holding on to trillions of dollars in cash?

If they were true American people; would they not want to invest in the country that made them rich in the first place? All these in your face conundrums are the driving force for the current 99% movement.

The G.O.P. and the Tea Party are one and the same. They had the white house for almost a decade and look what has happened.

The GOP hides behind our flag when they are actual charlatans and snake oil salesman. ALEC, the heritage foundation is being run by Bush war criminals. The real reason this country and other countries around the world are having detrimental crisis is FEAR itself.

Just as Martin Luther King said "all we have to fear is fear itself." Our government used 911 to wage this war to end democracy itself little by little. The U.S. government fell right into it as Bin Laden and the Saudi sheiks want us to believe.

What ever oil less countries that have banking and other American ties are suffering needlessly right now. This must be part of a plan that went south. Although China and Brazil are laughing at us right now and want to take the lead from U.S.

All the while we are policing the whole world!

We need not fear but fear itself no mater what happens to the U.S. "we the people" shall always prevail.

I love this country dearly that is why I am talking about the problems we have in a broader light. I also have some great reasons to fix our problems we now have. These created from years of extraction and in your face corruption.

We still have the fairest country of all "as crazy as that sounds lately." The problem is that everyone with a half decent education can see that. It takes some nerve to say that the people who are the backbone of America the 99% are mobs?

Did we say that about the Koch brother made up Tea Party movement that is only crushing democracy itself? The Tea Party ideology is plain in you face communalism!

The Tea Party folks want you to believe socialism is bad. Like Brad Pitt Said Quote"socialism is not as bad as the Tea Party makes you want to believe" Unquote.

France for example is a socialist country. The government is as fair as could be for a small country. People seem to be happy and if they are not they take to the streets. Somehow changes or compromises are made to rectify the problem whatever it is.

However in a communist country like China you can't have the babies you want or you can't have a say in anything! Government or even say what you want. Or write an honest book like this one. No say whatsoever in your local government ECT... the differences are there to see and they have a master plan as the Tea Party has. The master plan is to ultimately give NO SAY to Joe the plumber!

Now dead Bin Laden grew up watching a wide expanse of poverty all around him the fortunate one. Even though his father was a contractor as I was he was brought up in a privileged life.

Bin Laden's father built the road to Jordan that people said for years could not be done. As far as I know he did not come from blue blood but the family did work and have royal Friends.

Mecca is a place that Mohamed decided to make a religion. This in the location where he witnessed the falling of asteroids. Mohamed was married to a very rich widow. This marriage gave him the time and money needed to write the Koran "the Islamic version of the written bible."

Now centuries later Bin Laden's father also built the black granite stone building in the middle of Mecca. He used those sacred asteroids that came down to visit Mohamed's town. This is also the site where the building was built on.

Mecca brings in just about the same stream of money as the Saudis oil industry. It is written in the Koran that the trip to Mecca is fundamental and a mandatory pilgrimage of the Muslim faith if you have the means to do so. The Saudi's paid for and had the black stone Holy site building in the middle of Mecca built.

I respect everyone's right to religion any religion. I just don't think it was necessary to attack our country. The Saudi's and other Muslim nations have a problem with Democracy itself. It is the religious fanatics that are brainwashed or just crazy with FEAR and religious LIES! The Muslim countries created these modern day religious wars by there terrorist plots. This only created hate and many needless deaths and casualties in religions name.

Evangelicals, Mormons, Christians, Catholics and all other denominations should and maybe condemned for causing death and destruction to Gods lands in the end.

Using religious beliefs to kill and take over countries. We should just let god deal with religious wars in his normal ways "not war." Wars have been produced throughout our world's history. Apparently we humans have not yet learned something from history.

The last honest American elections were Jimmy Carters election in 1976. They did not have to raise money for him and his running mates. They used the IRS money; you know that little box on the right corner that says 3 dollars go to the presidential election campaign.

We need to go back to using just that for the election process. Television time should be free as the many hours of news." If it can't buy a lot of commercials so what, the debates and every thing political should be all free."

If the current rederick full debates were ended and our country's real problems were debated we would not be in the huge mess. Our Country faces many problems today could have been averted.

If CSU Stanislaus and Sac State and U.C. Davis, Penn State and many other Campus administrations. "If they did their jobs properly and ran their schools properly." Many current problems and of many thousands of students, just like me would not have had a problem at all in school.

This county should not want to end up like the island of Rhodes in the Greek islands. We also need to over haul this war machine government along with education and the banking system. These fifteen steps should help immediately. Only if we all come together and demand our government to have them implemented. Now not in ten or more years!

First of all we need to ban Nixon, oops I mean Norquist from politics making his pledge end now! It expires in 2013 any way.

Second; we need to implement new and old guidelines that worked in the past and were taken away by special interests over the past thirty years.

Third; As Dylan Ratigan advocates very well. We need to get the money out of politics.

Forth; we need reform and reorganize the banking system. So that the banking failures that happened in 1930's and again in 2008 don't happen again and again because we overlooked the in your face problem. "Mostly for the middle class and under privileged citizens"

Fifth; we should give the same tax incentives that Bush and Dick administration gave to the manufactures to leave this country. This should get them to come back purchase and retool the 50,000 factories that were closed.

All this destabilizing, deregulating, and very disruptive man made laws is strangling to our country's economy. The very corrupt G.O.P. administrations that held the law making power for many years. This by scaring the citizens of the united states into Tea Party type fabrications.

Sixth; we need to tell China that they need to write off at least half our Debt NOW! As we did to other nations in the past. Not to mention to pay for the manipulation of there own currency they have gotten away with for many years now.

Seventh; we need to lower the U.S. Corporation Tax by at least five Percent or more.

Eighth; we need to put a small percentage fee on every export transaction we make to put in our coffers. Our "made in America" products are worth paying double even triple of what a "made in China" product is worth. The American made products last double or triple then the time a similar product that was made in China.

Ninth; we need to start building technology based and manufacturing factories here in America in a green way. This so our intellectual patents don't become all made in China. We can't just say it will cost the corporation less to make it is worth less in quality also.

Tenth; we need to spend the same amount of money that we invested in a made up ten + year's long war at least three trillion dollars, and invest it in the big nation building and infrastructure in the United States. Also tax incentives for job creating endeavors that made U.S. grow in the past population increases.

Eleventh; we need to close a few bases around the world starting with Germany this money can be used to strengthen our current and newer fleet. A couple strategic bases around the world are plenty.

Twelfth; we need to reverse META LAWS, Each city should put a bill together for the taxes due on a foreclosure and the fees taken by the META laws and send them to the banks that own them. Instead they sale at a fraction and that lowers the taxes for the cities also.

Thirteenth; we need to stop giving billions of our tax dollars to countries that need other necessities. Whatever the country needs humanitarian relief. In the form of what they need not money. That mostly never ends up fixing the initial problem.

We as a country need to stop giving our money away thinking it will solve the underlying problems we face in today's world. In fact by giving huge amounts of money every time we go to war; this in itself causes wars to start purposely for the money even though no government we have recently gone to war with will admit it.

Fourteenth; if oil is the reason for the multiple wars and greenhouse gases. Why can't we start making steam engine cars again and use our fossil fuels for Flying and a few other areas. I love this country and we all deserve a better future and I know we can turn it around we just have to overhaul our wasteful and needless spending without a real plan.

Fifteenth; Religion and Religious organizations need to stay out of government altogether and governments need to stay out of religion. Same goes with sex and a woman's uterus!

I have yet to get an answer from Gov. Jerry Brown's office. The son of Gov. Pat Brown one of the founders of the "California master plan for higher Education" of 1960 I was exposing a major budget problem I thought.

He said "it was easier to govern this state this time around?   One would never think that an educational system can be as corrupt an unmoral as all the schools in question. Where are the concerns for the very people who they are supposed to nurture and teach on a daily bases.

I never thought the administration of a school would be so diabolical and corrupt. Then I read about Fernald and the Penn State, Kent state and U.C Davis student un-American incidents. I know we can fix our current democracy and economy oriented problems. We just need to come together and plan then implement!

Truth is that every problem has a solution. Doing the morally right things is all we have to do. That in it self will fix "in time" all things that are now out of control.

The G.O.P. and the Tea Party already had our credit rating down graded needlessly with their obstructionisms and brinkmanship. They show that they really don't care about this country or anyone in it.

It is obnoxious and only obvious when you sit down and hear the do nothing rederick. In all the resent GOP Presidential debates about the U.S. future. Then distract from the real issues the attacks and worry about abortion when we need good working government structures.

I love this country, even after all that has happened to me here. Even the Newtster wants to get poor kids to work?

How about Furnald type schools and institutions again! Mitt Romney and Newt, Cain, Palin, Perry, Bachman as GOP Presidential hopefuls in 2012?   OMG!

 And we ended up with Mitt the billionaire who publicly said $300,000 is nothing to him! Approximately the same as the salary of the President of United States of America!

Let's get started and change this collision course now! "All I wanted was fairness in our democracy and my educational investments worth' and a real chance for that more illusive ladder of success." They only made me an advocate for real change and awareness to corruptions!

The last time I was arrested was at the Lacey's front door of the house I helped them save. That was over fifteen years ago. CSU and this attack on my rights have me very scared. I also wrote to the DA and explained the situation. They are going to add thousands of dollars to budget deficit on the special prosecution of myself anyway.

Mark Meckler co writer of Tea Party Patriots took a gun on board a plane "a fifteen year sentence." The same as Jailed recent pilot and politically connected tea party mike gets $250.00 fine "is that fair"? Clearly there are two sets of rules in our justice system and certainly no accountability for the people responsible for the start of our down fall! They currently are in other high banking and government jobs!

"The definition of crazy is doing the same things over again and expecting a different out come!"

THE END

The non fiction genre is what keeps the brain informed. Living through a situation, doing the due diligences and tireless research is necessary to articulate a true story on paper. Many years studying Lititutre and strongly believing in the truth of a mater. It is just as credible as having a degree in Lititutre or the subject being written about. Feedback Welcome what is your educational story?

Book Feedback TEAPARTY-UNIVERSITY.COM, RGD

www.ingramcontent.com/pod-product-compliance
Lightning Source LLC
Chambersburg PA
CBHW070002300526
45794CB00001B/151